SALES REENGINEERING FROM THE OUTSIDE IN

ENGAGING CUSTOMERS WITH A NEW APPROACH TO SALES, MARKETING, AND SERVICE

MARK BLESSINGTON

BILL O'CONNELL

McGraw-Hill, Inc.
New York San Francisco Washington, D.C. Auckland Bogotá
Caracas Lisbon London Madrid Mexico City Milan
Montreal New Delhi San Juan Singapore
Sydney Tokyo Toronto

Library of Congress Cataloging-in-Publication Data

Blessington, Mark.
    Sales reengineering from the outside in : engaging customers with
a new approach to sales, marketing, and service / Mark Blessington,
Bill O'Connell.
        p.   cm.
    Includes index.
    ISBN 0-07-005950-0 (hardcover)
    1. Selling—Case studies.   2. Marketing—Case studies.
I. O'Connell, Bill II. Title.
HF5438.25.B566 1995
658.8′1—dc20   95-16097
                                                         CIP

1 2 3 4 5 6 7 8 9 0 DOC/DOC 9 0 0 9 8 7 6 5

ISBN 0-07-005950-0

*The sponsoring editor for this book was James Bessent, the editing
supervisor was Jane Palmieri, and the production supervisor was Donald
Schmidt. It was set in Fairfield by Terry Leaden of McGraw-Hill's
Professional Book Group composition unit.*

Printed and bound by R. R. Donnelley & Sons Company.

This book is printed on recycled, acid-free paper
containing a minimum of 50% recycled, de-inked fiber.

For Cindy and Phyl

CONTENTS

ACKNOWLEDGMENTS

We wish to thank all of our partners and colleagues at Sibson & Company, but especially:

Dave Kuhlman, for his timely and brilliant interventions to stabilize the content and storyline of the book. We always knew if Dave liked it, we were past our toughest and best critic.

Lisa Marchese, for her patient listening and reshaping of the initial themes and diagnostic tools outlined in the book. Lisa's work on how changes in procurement capabilities are scrambling how firms will need to sell in the future became an underlying foundation for our thinking.

Lisa Hankin and Len Nowakowski, for their incisive editing; Steve Strelsin, for his support throughout the process; and Ron Brandsdorfer, for his tireless efforts and coordination with McGraw-Hill.

Kathy Smith, for her unending work in typing, proofreading, and keeping only one master copy in circulation; Felicia Alexander, for her personal sacrifices to ensure we made our deadlines; and Sunday Whitaker, for her style and flair in text and graphics.

Special thanks goes to Fay Hansen, our editor, whose commitment and work ethic kept the momentum going when we went off to work with clients.

Mark Blessington
Bill O'Connell

INTRODUCTION

This book is about how executives can build revenue and profitability by better managing the process through which firms exchange value with customers.

We see a tumultuous world in sales and marketing giving rise to a call for "outside-in" or customer-based reengineering. The first generation of reengineering had a mixed track record. With this book, we explore the new world of procurement and provide a second generation of tools for reengineering and managing for enduring and profitable relationships with customers.

TROUBLE IN SALES AND MARKETING

Buyers have taken the upper hand with sales.

Buyers know much more than they did just a few years ago. Their information systems tell them far more than the monthly reports salespeople use. They now can measure the cost of owning the supplier's products down to inventory turns and return on a square foot of warehouse space. The buyer's assessment standards are so refined, and their coordination with their internal customers is so well developed, that buyers have multidimensional statistics for quantifying supplier performance. Gone are the days when sellers knew more than buyers.

Buyers have changed the rules of the game. They are reducing their sources of supply. They are creating single-sourcing arrangements. They are even managing global partnerships and providing supplies to their suppliers. Gone are the days when salespeople could explain the company's program for next year and, on the same day, walk out with a commitment for the following year.

Buyers have a respected place at the executive table. They are viewed as critical to overall business success, especially since they manage such a great portion of a company's costs. They have the internal power to set the rules and make suppliers stick to them. Gone are the days when purchasing rules and procedures could be circumvented by securing orders directly with the buyer's internal customers.

Buyers have also turned the marketer's world upside down.

Buyers are demanding a new approach to marketing. They are doing their own advertising, but they are making suppliers pay for it. They are demanding everyday promotional pricing and are not grateful for the occasional good deal. They are dictating which channels of distribution they will use and which specific company representatives they want to work with. They want each marketing program to be tailored to their unique situation. They even demand that special products be created just for them.

Gone are the days when the customer came to the company—now the company must go to the customer.

THE CALL FOR OUTSIDE-IN REENGINEERING

One response to these and a host of other sales and marketing problems is to bring costs in line with lower sales or margins. The popularity of this tactic can be seen by reading the business press, where reports of one massive layoff are being eclipsed by the next in a matter of days. For example, the pharmaceutical industry cut 3 percent of its workforce between June and October of 1994 (*Crain's New York Business*, December 5, 1994). For some firms, these initiatives may lead to short-term improvements. But competitors are quick to match, if not better, cost take-outs, thus negating initial competitive benefits.

Other firms have focused a decade of attention on their production, design, or logistical operations and still have not reached industry leadership positions. The remaining bottleneck to achieving leadership is creating breakthroughs in how customers are found, grown, and sustained.

Reengineering is tailor-made for dealing with the customer/supplier relationship. Its focus on process aligns with the quality initiatives that have driven purchasing to where it is today. Its emphasis on radical, out-of-the-box thinking introduces the potential for improvements that will not easily be copied by competitors. And, its embrace of technology offers hope that suppliers can regain even footing in the age of information.

To the extent that an organization can stabilize its customer base, it can improve its decision-making capabilities. By reducing customer churn, a company can build its resources with the confidence that comes from standing on a firm foundation. For example, if 60 percent of a firm's net income comes from a stable customer base, it has a better chance of recouping its investments due to its more reliable future than a firm where only 30 percent of its net income is derived from predictable customer revenue.

There are two primary reasons to reengineer the core processes through which suppliers search, acquire, build, and sustain relationships with their prospects and customers. The first is to provide the kind of product offerings that buyers want and need. The second is to lock up profitable customer commitments and lock out competitive threats by making the switch-out cost of the relationship unacceptably high.

By the year 2000, we predict that, in addition to balance statements and income statements, companies will be able to develop financial statements which reflect the health and stability of their customer bases. To do this, firms will have to project the income stream from those contractual and long-standing customer relationships which represent 50 percent or more of the profitability of the firm. A short time after that, such pro formas will be a requirement to qualify for top-grade credit and investment rankings.

PROBLEMS WITH FIRST-GENERATION REENGINEERING

Reengineering now has been in use long enough to tally some initial results. In too many cases, the results are disappointing. By one estimate, 75 percent of these first-generation reengineering efforts have fallen short of the goals set for them (*Management Review*, June 1994). Even James Champy, in his second book, *Reengineering Management* (1995), cites a study which found that cost reduction and market share growth goals were missed by as much as 30 percent.

The key problems we have observed with the first generation of reengineering efforts are the exclusion of sales, the anticipation and management of intermediate declines in performance, the use of cookbook solutions, and resistance to radical change. Each of these causes is now examined in more detail.

WHERE IS SALES?

While there are a number of explanations for the problems that have been experienced with reengineering, perhaps the most instructive cause is excluding sales from reengineering, which a large number of firms have chosen to do. Initially, firms seemed willing to reengineer practically anything but the functional area that has the greatest responsibility for finding and minding customers.

The same problem occurred with the quality movement. Quality efforts pursued significant improvements in manufacturing and behind-the-scenes customer support functions. As we now know from numerous surveys and studies, the results of many of these quality initiatives were mixed as well. While the quality concepts were sound, financial impact often faltered.

We see a brutally simple parallel between problems with the quality movement and those with first-generation reengineering: *It does not pay to leave sales out of initiatives aimed at driving improved customer satisfaction or profitability.*

Reengineering that seeks to improve company performance without including sales and other customer-facing positions is missing a big piece of the picture. Sales and marketing have too much impact on the firm's customer effectiveness not to be included in reengineering efforts. Reengineering for better product is not enough, because customers are all too aware that they buy much more than a product. Customers are buying solutions and applications, and the supplier's representatives they deal with on a day-to-day basis determine whether or not the customer's purchases produce the targeted impact on performance.

But let's be honest. There is a good reason for not including sales: Working with customers is messy. The customer interface is the last bastion to resist the quality and reengineering movements. It is the area where:

- Results can be recorded but not predicted, analyzed but not forecast.
- Technocrats, consultants, and engineers fear to tread because customers don't always cooperate with management theories or brilliant analytical prescriptions.
- The rational engineer and the scientific manager are forced onto the slippery surface of working with customers.

Customers are inconsistent and disloyal as often as they are deliberate and directed. Salespeople are a different breed—lone rangers threatening to take their customers with them should the company get any radical ideas that could impact their commission earnings. In combination, salespeople and customers have appeared to be too much for the science of reengineering. We want this to change.

The Valley of Despair

Another cause for reengineering shortfalls is underestimating the "valley of despair"—that infamous drop in performance that all too often accompanies radical organizational renovations. Either the valley is not anticipated, or it is longer or deeper than anticipated. This problem haunted most large-scale organization change initiatives of the past, and, unfortunately, reengineering is no exception. In fact, because of the radical objectives of first-generation reengineering efforts, the valley of despair has frightened companies into suboptimizing their reengineering goals and ambitions.

Cookbook Solutions

Another cause of reengineering failure has been the use of cookbook solutions. For example, reengineering efforts guided by sociotech gurus tend to look alike. In one such case, two large companies in different industries (leasing and financial planning) and with different reengineering objectives both ended up with "coordinating systems" and "operating systems" as critical elements of their design recommendations. One of these companies is now in the awkward position of redesigning the design because these generic organization structure concepts were not aligned with the realities of managing a sales force.

Reengineering itself is not a strategy to achieve competitive advantage. It is a management tool to use as part of a broader business strategy designed to reach competitive advantage. Reengineering is too often claimed to be effective in and of itself, rather than as a tool used to achieve other objectives. It is possible to reengineer group processes, for example, for faster cycle times. But faster cycle times and lower costs don't necessarily fit into customer requirements for coping in the real world. And traditional reengineering does not revolutionize the measures used to evaluate enduring customer effectiveness, much less accommodate the full range of sometimes emotional behavior which accompanies customer buying habits.

RESISTANCE TO RADICAL CHANGE

The last category of first-generation reengineering failures is attributable to the term "radical." On one hand, the radical challenge issued by reengineering creates the opportunity to gain a competitive edge. On the other hand, people do not change radically; they evolve. Thus, if reengineering leaders believe their radical vision of a brave new world can be implemented quickly, employees are sure to prove them wrong. And, indeed, they have.

It is unrealistic to expect people dramatically and fundamentally to change how they perform a job in a short period of time. First-generation reengineers hoped that a cross-functional, multilevel systems approach to change would eliminate much of the resistance to change experienced by more traditional change programs. Their presumption was that if the system was redesigned and people were well educated about the new design, then people quickly would be enabled and empowered to perform the newly reengineered processes.

One of the classic causes of failure in changing an organization—"the transplant the body rejects"—is better managed by the reengineering design process than by traditional change programs. It incorporates cross-functional and multilevel involvement. Still, everyone can't be on the design team, so a significant not-made-here syndrome still develops once the team concludes its work and its members resume their everyday tasks.

A SECOND GENERATION

In the wake of mounting publicity about failed efforts, first-generation reengineers have issued caveats and qualified their statements. They continue to issue a call to arms to take risks, but they are starting to recognize the organizational and technical difficulties stemming from radical change efforts.

We propose a second generation of reengineering that focuses outside on the customers and their procurement processes.

Second-generation reengineering is based on three key principles that distinguish it from first-generation efforts.

Principle 1: Focus on the Customer/Supplier Relationship

The customer/supplier relationship is the focus of second-generation reengineering. This calls for including sales, marketing,
customer service, and other positions that have regular and substantial contact with the customer. But more importantly, it also
means starting with the customer and working backwards. We
refer to this as "outside-in" reengineering, or aligning a company's sales, marketing, and service processes with customer procurement processes.

A significant potential impact of outside-in reengineering is
examining all the process flows between the supplier and the
customer. Customers are frustrated with fragmented interactions
where the right hand doesn't know what the left hand is doing.
Outside-in reengineering can find solutions that create seamless
interactions across functions. A good example is AT&T's reengineering of its sales, marketing, and support services personnel
for its global information systems division into 560 worldwide
customer-focused teams.

A thorough understanding of customer procurement processes is mandatory in outside-in reengineering. Current and future
improvements in procurement capabilities must be mapped so
that alignments can be forged with the company's customer
management processes. One sure way to gain this customer
insight is to include customers as members of the reengineering
design team.

Principle 2: Balance Revolutionary Vision with Evolutionary Execution

The second principle is to formulate a revolutionary vision but to
implement that vision in an evolutionary manner through continuous improvement. This approach requires a fundamental

rethinking of critical business processes that will ultimately yield dramatic improvements in results, but it acknowledges the fundamental reality that people change gradually. As a result:

1. The firm sets more realistic expectations for how much change can be accomplished in a given period of time.

2. The reengineering program uses quick wins to achieve significant short-term gains while maintaining momentum and enthusiasm for the overall new design. For example, specific groups of customers are targeted for initial implementation.

3. The program uses broader involvement in design to extend implementation commitment.

4. The valley of despair is not as deep because change is designed to occur within the context of ongoing operations, rather than as a one-time flip of the switch that engenders significant disruption of day-to-day sales and customer service requirements.

PRINCIPLE 3: MELD ART AND SCIENCE

The inclusion of the customer/supplier interface in second-generation reengineering requires a melding of art and science. The terms "art" and "science" are used here to illustrate the tremendous differences between first- and second-generation reengineering, between internal processes and buyer/supplier relations, and between relatively predictable processes and inherently unpredictable processes.

We draw on art for understanding. Understanding customers is really more of an art than a science. No function is more aware of this reality than the sales function, and, ultimately, this one-to-one uniqueness defies science. A sense of art is required to grasp the customer's need for comfort, reassurance, relationship, and commitment. Sometimes these needs are met by illusion, sometimes by manipulation, sometimes by glad-handing, sometimes on the golf course, sometimes by reference checks.

We may not like it and we may not admit it, but we cannot reengineer the customer's human wiring. We can only improve the art of listening, of empathizing, and of delivering on the spirit of what we promise.

We draw on science for courage. Design teams, interviews, focus groups, surveys, process maps, strategic alternatives, new terms and definitions...these and other reengineering tools will help us take the art of selling to a new and higher level. Executives seeking a place on the plateau of excellence must join the best efforts of reengineering with the life lessons from the artistry of selling. Merging the science of reengineering with the murky alchemy of sales is a goal which will take the next decade to complete—but the path is getting clearer each day.

THE OUTSIDE-IN PERSPECTIVE

The new competitive requirements companies now face are part of much broader changes in the global economy. Times of significant change require leaders to rethink how they spend their time and how to reinvent their organizations on an almost continuous basis. The first and most critical step in the movement to world-class supplier status is scrapping the inside-out perspective of the old sales model, which presumes that growth derives from proactive selling. Instead, managers must clearly articulate customer procurement needs and processes. Powered with this understanding, it is possible to harness the accumulated expertise of marketing, sales, service, and support functions. Companies can reorient themselves from the cool reserve required for cost cutting to the superheated concentration required for customer breakthroughs.

Managing this task while assuring that sales results meet budget goals each quarter is a daunting challenge. To help, we have created a time management rule specifically for executives in the midst of customer-driven reengineering. This rule, which we call the 40/40/20 rule, calls for executives to spend:

- 40 percent of their time on looking *outside* the firm, at customers and competitors

- 40 percent of their time looking *inside* the firm at designing, communicating, and executing the changes necessary to align the firm with customer needs

- 20 percent of their time *realigning* the support systems necessary for others to execute their responsibilities with excellence

The 40/40/20 concept is a broad framework for securing the time required to form new relationships with customers. It also is a concrete rule for coordinating and energizing the firm's customer-coverage positions. Following the process detailed in this book requires looking outside the firm to customer needs, procurement practices, and competitive conditions; looking inside the firm to make the necessary adjustments in the firm's accumulated research/design/marketing/sales/service/logistics capability; and then aligning the support systems to help employees execute their tasks in ways that meet world-class standards.

The organization of this book reflects the 40/40/20 rule. The first part focuses on the world of the customer and the new competitive environment. The second part focuses on internal changes: reengineering the firm to infuse differential competitive advantage into the processes for identifying, acquiring, and exchanging the value required for profitable and sustained customer relationships. The third and final part deals with building the support systems required by those employees who must block and tackle on the front lines with customers every day.

The work presented here is based on the efforts of our clients—real people wrestling with real situations across the global economy.* Our clients over the years have ranged across all sizes, industries, and regions, bringing a universal quality to

---

*An important source of research for this book was a series of seminars titled *Sales Force 2000*, conducted by the authors and other members of Sibson & Company. These brainstorming sessions focused on anticipating the future of sales and what sales managers need to do in response.

the trends and solutions we discuss in this book. Virtually all of the executives we have worked with anticipate increasing the number and/or skills of those employees who bring different expertise and perspectives to the challenge of customer coverage, and seek new approaches to finding, minding, and serving customers over the next few years. Without exception, they believe that technology will continue to have a dramatic impact on the traditional sales process. And all agree that they must deliver higher levels of customer service tomorrow simply to retain the same level of loyal and profitable customers that they enjoy today.

ONE

LOOKING
OUTSIDE

The first section of this book focuses on the buying process and
how the dynamic of buying and selling has changed
dramatically over a short period of time. Sales and marketing
executives have not dedicated enough serious attention to this
subject—we have yet to find a book on buying or procurement
in the office of a sales or marketing executive. Furthermore, initial
reengineering efforts have shied away from reworking the process
of serving customers. These gaps need to close, and the first
step begins with looking at how customers are starting to conduct
their procurement processes.

CHAPTER	SUMMARY
1 The Power Shift	Power at the point of sale has shifted from the seller to the buyer. Factors such as technological proliferation, global competition, information technology, and the quality movement have increased the sophistication of buyers, and traditional sales and marketing approaches are losing effectiveness. The fact that customers have significantly improved their procurement capabilities is forcing more companies, in turn, to reengineer their approach to winning and keeping customers.

(Continued)

CHAPTER	SUMMARY
2 The New Procurement	Procurement expenditures are an increasingly significant portion of a company's costs. Procurement strategies now seek to reduce the number of suppliers the customer works with, building longer-lasting supplier relationships and pursuing single-source arrangements.
3 Models of Procurement	The quality movement and reengineering initiatives have driven today's buyers to manage the procurement *process* as aggressively as they manage *price*. This chapter provides a modern procurement model, and reviews how suppliers are evaluated today. We also trace the evolution of buying by examining earlier buying models. These models offer companies a framework for studying procurement in their own industries.

THE POWER SHIFT

As this chapter will explore, professional selling as we know it has existed in the United States for roughly 100 years. For about 90 of those 100 years, suppliers played a proactive role in the marketplace, selling what they made or created to relatively reactive customers. But beginning in the 1970s and accelerating through the 1980s and especially in the 1990s, a number of forces combined to shift the balance of power at the point of sale from suppliers to buyers. These forces were set loose by rapid advancements in information and communications technology. Meanwhile, suppliers continued to feel the constant need to reduce costs and meet the rising quality expectations of the customers.

The consequence of this power shift in negotiating capability at the point of sale has been constant margin erosion and a significant drop in many firms' abilities to forecast the likely return of reinvestments into their core businesses. The power shift places many executives in a dilemma that can only be resolved either by accepting this new reality and then trying to recapture some of the power, or by learning to operate more effectively with less power. Understanding the power shift to the purchaser from the seller is a crucial first step in recreating and sustaining profitable customer relationships.

THE OLD SALES MODEL

Selling first arose as a distinct and valued function within a modern business organization in the last quarter of the nineteenth century, in response to greatly expanded output from new mass-production industries. Periodic gluts of unsold goods prompted manufacturers to end their reliance on wholesalers, to concentrate on market share, and to develop their own sales and marketing functions. The first modern sales organizations, with sales offices based in major cities and run by sales managers, were in place by the turn of the century. At the National Cash Register company, the first professionally trained and managed sales force rose to prominence in the first two decades of this century. The machinery necessary for mass distribution grew hand in hand with the growth of mass production. Procter & Gamble, still cited today for its superior sales and marketing management, was one of the first companies to distribute products nationally through a network of branch sales offices.

As technological advances increasingly allowed manufacturers to make products at previously unthinkable volume levels, marketing and distribution departments became necessary for creating and sustaining the mass markets which absorbed the output. In some industries, such as agricultural machinery and office equipment, a sales force was required not only to distribute the new output levels, but also to market products that were increasingly complicated and costly. The size and complexity of the national and sometimes international organizations required to market and distribute products became a substantial barrier to entry in many industries by the turn of the century.

Throughout the eighties, many industries still pursued this strategy (that is, forming a large organization) by acquiring small firms. Evidence of companies who continue to form mass-market sales and distribution barriers include the food industry (for example, Nestlé's acquisition of Carnation, Kraft's acquisition of General Foods), commercial furniture (for example, Westinghouse's acquisition of Knoll, Reff, and Shaw-Walker), and such regional banking powerhouses as Banc One and Wachovia. Such acquisitions were frequently fueled by distribution synergies. From the salesperson's perspective, these acquisitions provided an opportunity to sell a broader assortment of products. From the new, larger firm's perspective, it meant gaining broader distribution of products with previously limited exposure. In all of these examples, companies were leveraging or cross-selling new products into larger, mass customer bases.

THE IMPACT OF MARKETING

The domination of business management by the sales function was moderated by the emergence of marketing in the 1950s and 1960s. In essence, marketing saved companies from repeatedly making products that salespeople had thought would sell, but ultimately had limited sales potential. Marketing moved away from writing copy or hiring talent that was "exciting" toward innovations such as focus groups, psychographics, and analyses of reach and frequency. Product pricing shifted from what customers would pay to what was required to make a profit. Marketing added a critical and previously missing science centered around defining customer needs, estimating market sizes, and managing product profitability.

From one perspective, the impact of marketing on selling was profound. Marketing was a separate function incorporating an analytical and financial perspective with a scientific intelligence about customer preferences. At first, marketing fought with sales on equal ground, with the top sales and marketing executives reporting to the CEO. Within a decade or less, sales was reporting to marketing in many corporations, and sales' organizational primacy was gone.

LAGGING BEHIND

From another perspective, after almost a century of experience in managing the selling function, remarkably little has changed.

Selling is predominantly transaction-oriented. Salespeople never lose sight of the purchase order, customers are viewed as personal properties, and long-term considerations seldom take precedence over the immediate need for sales credit. Manipulation can still be the implicit modus operandi, with salespeople using interpersonal relationships to secure business that otherwise would go to competitors. Many salespeople claim to have adopted concepts such as "consultative," "strategic," and "partnership" selling. But too often, these terms are merely clichés. Indeed, the Willy Lomans and Tin Men are still at large in many of today's sales forces.

Not only has sales held onto many of its tried and true approaches, but, also, marketing has not evolved adequately. If marketing had recognized that customer needs had extended far beyond product features, it would have seen that its customers were increasingly less satisfied. Nothing has been more embarrassing to the marketing profession than reminders of how important a role customer service can play in a firm's success. It exposed the marketers' blind spot: They had forgotten one of the classic *four P*s. They were immersed in the science surrounding *product, price*, and *promotion*. But the last *P, place*, where the company touches the customer, was lost in the shuffle. This is what the quality movement spelled out all too clearly. Both large and small American businesses had lost touch with their customers at a grass-roots level. They had become too enamored with the thought that the mass-market road to success was the one best way to competitive advantage.

Spurred on by the quality movement, companies have learned to manufacture using flexible batch production. Although mass-manufacturing operations no longer drive the U.S. economy, mass-distribution thinking still rules in the marketing and sales arms of most firms. Flexible marketing and sales and service processes, able to anticipate and adjust to the increasingly complex and rapidly changing demands of customer procurement processes, still do not exist in most firms.

THE PROMINENCE OF PURCHASING

The development of purchasing has taken an entirely different direction. The purchasing function in many firms has been reborn as the proactive party in buyer/seller relationships. This newly aggressive mode of purchasing has been referred to as *proactive purchasing* or *reverse marketing* in an effort to describe a procurement strategy that initiates and controls relations with suppliers. Other new strategies for procurement include basic partnering, expanded partnering, comakership, strategic alliances, and coalitional relationships.

It is also important to realize that purchasing has emerged as a more respected function within the corporate arena. Historically, the purchasing department was an isolated group considered to be the backwaters of management. Top executive careers typically did not include a stint in purchasing, and executives from other functional areas were reluctant to accept an assignment there. Simply put, purchasing was not part of the senior management team. A notable exception, of course, was retailing, where purchasing has always been a more prominent function.

Now, however, purchasing has come into its own. A recent Center for Advanced Purchasing Studies (CAPS) survey of CEOs and Presidents from *Fortune* 500 firms found that 65 percent view the purchasing function as very important to the overall success of the firm. This may be most evident in the automotive industry, where more effective purchasing is showing itself to be one of the most powerful ways to enhance profitability. Volkswagen did not pursue GM's best designer, division president, or CFO, but instead set its sights on GM's head of purchasing, Julio Ignacio Lopez. Indeed, GM's subsequent outcry at the loss of Lopez was confirmation of purchasing's prominence.

The migration of purchasing to the forefront has been initiated by a variety of factors, including technology, outsourcing, globalization, mergers and acquisitions, cost pressures, and customer quality expectations. The following sections will explore these areas in more detail.

TECHNOLOGY

Technology has had a substantial impact on the balance of power between suppliers and buyers. There are four components of technology's impact: technological proliferation, the volume and speed of communications, market information, and the impact of informed customers.

TECHNOLOGICAL PROLIFERATION

Part of the power shift from suppliers to buyers is due to the broad technology trends that affect virtually every company today. First, there is the tremendous rate of technological innovation. Companies must constantly adopt new and enhanced technology to maintain competitive product features. The pace of technological change is so pronounced that product life cycles have been shortened. Companies compete on the basis of speed, or how quickly they can bring innovations to market. In the past, new innovations were carefully assessed in terms of how they would cannibalize existing products. Now, cannibalization is not nearly as relevant as staying in the game; companies are left behind if they do not constantly introduce new products or product features.

Technological imitation has also shifted power away from suppliers. Innovations by one company are copied more quickly than ever before through reverse engineering, whereby a competitor disassembles and studies the product, acquires construction knowledge, and then creates a production link to manufacture that product for their own company. Many Japanese electronics firms became masters of this in the 1960s and 1970s. So, not only is technology constantly evolving, but it has less impact as a competitive edge. The result, from a salesperson's perspective, is that the products being sold seldom sell themselves because of a technological advantage. Whether it's computer software, fax machines, or medical supplies, today's innovation is often tomorrow's me-too product. Few companies are able to compete for very long solely on the basis of the superiority of their products' technical features and benefits.

Given the realities of technological proliferation, few organizations are confident that superior technology positions will drive future success. Companies used to create a product advantage and then cruise for decades on the basis of that advantage. Few companies are cruising on product advantage today. Some firms keep trying to tweak the core product design, but often the sales force reports back that the product is unsellable based on only a 3 percent improvement in technology.

Instead, companies must recognize that technological proliferation has shifted power to buyers; it allows buyers to place suppliers on even ground and pit one supplier against another. Today, buyers demand more than technology. Because technological excellence has become a prerequisite for being in the business in the first place, customers have learned to choose suppliers based on other criteria. In most industries today, sophisticated buyers are demanding excellence throughout the entire sales and service cycle. Consequently, salespeople and other employees in customer-facing positions must add the missing innovation and differentiation: the competitive edge in today's marketplace. This is the soft side of competitiveness, ushered in by technological proliferation.

COMMUNICATION VOLUME AND SPEED

Nowhere is the rate of innovation so obvious or pronounced as in electronics and communications. The volume and speed of daily communications and the resulting pressure to respond is accelerating geometrically. Most sales executives are swimming in phone messages and faxes. The average workload of a sales force is increasing rapidly. Customers often don't wait for a sales visit to place their orders or ask for service. They leave voicemail messages, send faxes, use overnight delivery, or submit their orders on-line through direct computer links. Customer response procedures have to cover 24 hours a day. Leads flow into the sales force day and night.

The standard customer expectation is immediate service. In many cases, the supplier has less direct contact with the customer than ever before. EDI (Electronic Data Interchange, a system for networking two companies' data directly via computer), for example, is changing the way buyers and suppliers communicate. Although mailing and faxing are currently the most widely used communication forms, there are a growing number of EDI transactions. On average, companies use EDI for 8 percent of their purchases, with some industries' use as high as 30 percent (CAPS, 1993). And EDI is no longer used just for ordering. Companies use EDI to transmit a variety of information, including quotations, material scheduling, shipping dates, and order payments.

Again, buyers have used technology to take power in the buyer/seller exchange. Rather than using technology to accelerate ahead of buyers, many companies are struggling to keep up with buyers' demands for communication speed and responsiveness.

MARKET INFORMATION

Three-fourths of the sales executives we work with say that technology has increased the sophistication and capabilities of their buyers faster than it has improved the effectiveness of their sales forces. The buyer at Wal-Mart knows how many turns and how much profit he or she made on each brand as compared with every other brand in a given product category, with data updated on a day-by-day basis. Compare this with the salesperson across the desk who may only know last quarter's sales volume for his or her product line. The combination of personal computers and better cost accounting systems enables the buyer, in many industries, to know far more about the true long-term profit economics of the sale than the seller does.

Now, in many industries, the buyer not only understands the performance claims of numerous suppliers, but also understands the operating costs—costs that might accrue to the buying organization—in greater detail and in a more timely manner than the seller. Armed with new information technology, customers have access to comparative products and prices, and no longer rely on salespeople for market information. The buyer and seller in many industries today arrive at the negotiating table with unequal knowledge about the value of the buy. If knowledge is power, this battle must be won by more and more suppliers if the current trends are to be reversed.

Just a decade ago, as economies of scale and financial constraints drove many industries to consolidate, key and national account management became the latest sales strategy to handle the rapid centralization of buying points throughout America. In just 10 short years, suppliers have gone from one point—proclaiming effective national and key account relationship management, in conjunction with local area sales order taking, as the coming wave in the arsenal of selling techniques—to the point where, in several industries, face-to-face order taking itself has been replaced by EDI networks. Ordering decisions are becoming computer-driven as scanners allow ordering and planning without sales representative participation.

Sales used to be a fairly simple process of describing products to customers. Now, the sales force often constitutes a bottleneck in the process of buyer/supplier information exchange. The product information the customer needs is increasingly complex. Information about delivery, ordering, and logistics has become more important and complicated as buyers have started to understand the cost consequences of how they receive the product.

Normally, selling organizations rely on their sales force for market intelligence on competitors' and customers' needs. Other functions—pricing, R&D, manufacturing—often depend on the sales force for information about the customer. Sales forces without modern communications tools can wind up bottlenecking information in both directions. The information can neither get out from sales nor get into sales fast enough to produce the kind of customized products based on customer specifications that many markets require.

THE IMPACT OF INFORMED CUSTOMERS

Executives often fail to acknowledge that information technology distributes data equally to both the supplier and the customer. In many markets, salespeople can't convince customers to buy products for which sales has incomplete information. Many customers know more about the true performance of a supplier's product than the supplier. This is particularly true for consumer product firms.

Optical character recognition (OCR) technology allows buyers in the food retailing industry to understand transfer costs from food stores to customers. It also allows everyone in the supply chain to understand what it takes to get a product all the way from raw material out through the checkout counter. It's an industry in which many purchasing trends are at their furthest advancement because the information exchange technology is in place. The resulting impact on the suppliers' sales forces is a fascinating peek at the future for many other industries.

Twenty years ago, a salesperson called on the owner or the manager at a grocery store. Today, a salesperson with the same product line may find a buyer who is educated two years beyond an MBA and sitting behind reams of data. That person can tell the salesperson how much shaving cream sold yesterday at what price in the Topeka, Kansas, stores. He or she can also tell the salesperson that the supplier must meet quality requirements for managing shelf stock or lose shelf space in all of the distributor's 18,000-sq-ft stores. The buyer can negotiate the price based on several competitive pricing algorithms per foot of shelf space.

For sales forces in many industries, technology has increased the sophistication and capability of their buyers faster than it has been used to improve the effectiveness of their sales work. Previously, customers often relied on their suppliers for information about the product and for feedback on how to use the product, its competitive advantages, and its optional features. Now salespeople spend their customer-facing time explaining their firm's communications technologies, such as EDI, fax, bar coding, or CAD systems, to allow customers to gather information and intervene in the sales/service/supply process in ways that were never before possible. Customers can even use concurrent engineering through communications and information technologies to become involved in the production of supplies at the design stage—a rare event even seven years ago.

OUTSOURCING

While the impact of technology on the balance of power has been substantial, the power shift has been exacerbated by outsourcing. Historically, companies protected their innovations through patents on innovations they developed on their own. Now, companies use outsourcing as a key tactic for keeping pace with technological innovation—they introduce innovations to their customers by buying new technology from suppliers. The catch, however, is that those suppliers also sell the same technological innovations to competing companies, resulting in a vicious cycle of innovation followed by imitation.

Big companies like General Motors once assumed that they would make their own supplies and components. These same companies now assume that outsourcing is a logical answer to questions about the profit economics of their earlier make/buy decisions and their own operational costs. With the dramatic increase in outsourcing, procurement strategy takes on greater importance to a world-class manufacturer. According to some

PROCUREMENT SPENDING
AS A PERCENTAGE OF SALES

Industry	Procurement Spending as a Percentage of Sales
Automotive	61%
Carbon/Steel	58
Machinery	57
Chemicals	56
Appliances	53
Electrical Equipment	50
Paper	40
Construction	38
Electronics	37
Beverages	35
Computers	34
Pharmaceuticals	21
Personal Care Products	21
Telecommunications Services	16

Source: CAPS, 1993.

Figure 1-1

experts, 3 out of 10 large U.S. industrial companies outsource for more than half of their manufacturing needs.

Underlying all of this is the fact that, on average, procurement represents 50 percent of the operational expenses of *Fortune* 500 firms. As Figure 1-1 illustrates, there are industries in which procurement spending runs as high as 60 percent of sales. It is not surprising that intensive manufacturing firms tend to have a higher level of procurement spending as a percent of sales, given the quality and quantity of materials needed for production, than service and nonmanufacturing organizations.

Although buyers commonly bargain to shave purchase costs, most attempts to both reduce operational costs and ensure quality manufacturing results require purchasers to intervene upstream, in the suppliers' design, logistics, postsales service, and production decisions. As more firms start to understand their profit economics and to push costs beyond internal cost reduction efforts, the need to focus on procurement efficiency and effectiveness will accelerate.

GLOBALIZATION

In most industries, the relationship between customers and suppliers now occurs in the context of global markets. In many industries, U.S. suppliers face competition from foreign firms with lower costs, greater flexibility, and better quality. Globalized sourcing offers alternative sources of supply and fuels buyers' expectations for quality products at competitive prices. It inspires customers to revisit their supplier base and scrutinize products and prices in unprecedented ways. As more countries from Eastern Europe and the Pacific Rim enter the global marketplace, competition among suppliers will increase even more dramatically.

MERGERS AND ACQUISITIONS

Because of the merger and acquisition binge of the last decade, a greater percent of sales volume is now generated by fewer customers. In industries where the 80/20 rule applies (where 80 percent of sales volume is generated by 20 percent of the customers), the rule is becoming more pronounced as a result of mergers and acquisitions. Customers are getting larger, and larger customers have more power.

SHRINKING SUPPLIER BASE

Extensive surveys of *Fortune* 500 firms reveal a 5 percent average annual decrease in the number of active suppliers per *Fortune* 500 purchasing department. As Figure 1-2 illustrates, the decline in the average number of suppliers is occurring in many industries.

As the number of active suppliers declines, the survivors become more entrenched, and it becomes more costly for competitors to unseat incumbent suppliers. In this consolidated

ANNUAL DECLINE IN THE NUMBER OF SUPPLIERS 1990 – 1992	
Industry	Change in Number of Active Suppliers
Telecommunications Services	-4%
Carbon/Steel	-9
Pharmaceuticals	-5
Computers	-6
Paper	0
Machinery	-7
Beverages	-2
Electronics	-5
Construction	-3
Automotive	0
Personal Care Products	-7
Appliances	-5
Chemicals	-4
Electrical Equipment	-18
Source: CAPS, 1993.	

Figure 1-2

world for sources of supply, the obstacles to entry grow larger, as do the costs of entry. More and different expertise is required to help the sales force overcome these obstacles and convince the prospective customer that switching to a new supplier will yield a payoff for the customer.

COST PRESSURES

Throughout the 1980s, slow productivity growth, weak consumer demand, global competitiveness, and excess capacity put downward pressure on profits and encouraged heavy scrutiny of costs. The recessionary period of the late 1980s and early 1990s inspired a new focus on innovative procurement methods as a way to reduce costs, increase quality, and gain a competitive edge.

Until the mid- to late 1980s, the purchasing function was seen simply as a necessity of doing business. At best, it negotiated price discounts of 5 to 10 percent from suppliers. But companies are more often looking to modern-day procurement processes for 10 to 30 percent cuts in purchase, inventory, and operational costs.

CUSTOMER QUALITY EXPECTATIONS

A majority of large firms have embraced quality movements throughout their operations, using, for example, the Baldrige Award criteria. One of the biggest by-products of the quality movement is not what happens inside the firm, but how the movement sharpens the expectations of the external stakeholders in the firm's success: vendors, customers, and potential partners.

The quality movement has generated close scrutiny of product quality in all functions, including manufacturing, warehousing, and product development. The quality movement has also focused both buyers and suppliers on the value delivered to the end consumer. The push for a more complex and valuable exchange has come from customers because they have more thoroughly examined and measured the value of the products and services and are, therefore, in a better position to evaluate the performance claims that suppliers make about their products and services.

SOPHISTICATED EVALUATIONS

Quality expectations are increasingly important when there are fewer suppliers providing more products and services. Manufacturing firms in particular tend to use a more formal approach to measuring all their suppliers' quality, including assessments of supplier qualifications, supplier quality improvement efforts, and supplier certification. Customers evaluate the present level of several alternative suppliers' quality, choose to work with specific firms for quality improvement, and then certify the selected suppliers for dock-to-stock delivery contracts over long periods of time, rather than order by order.

One of the most significant impacts of the quality movement is the growing ability of many firms to measure performance and compare it with suppliers' performance claims. The quality movement, combined with the new information power of personal computers, has allowed customers to develop better assessments of true product and service performance, even more accurate than those of the supplier.

Customers now demand greater customization of their service protocols, EDI procedures, and logistical interfaces. In many cases, customers simply will not tolerate inspections, rework, returns, large inventories, and other time-consuming and expensive quality-related tasks. Constant attention to the quality demands and service requirements of a firm's customers and continued investments in technology provide the tools and support to meet minimal customer expectations, but few suppliers have found these efforts to be enough to sustain competitive advantage.

Many suppliers are having a delayed reaction to their customers' more aggressive demands because they are trapped in their inside-out perspective. Their primary source of market information is often the sales force, and their market intelligence is frequently skewed by their need to meet the demands of their own sales organization, management expectations, and reward systems. They don't recognize the proactive procurement stance that now characterizes the approach of many customers.

LONG-TERM VALUE

The old sales model assumes that a transaction is measured by its tangible economic value as reflected in the pricing and discounting strategies of the selling organization. In other words, the selling firm imposes its definition of a valuable transaction.

Yet customers are insisting that the proper measurement is not only the financial measure of the transaction but also the long-term value-added return of every transaction—the extent to which the transaction builds long-term wealth creation by evidencing greater quality to end-user consumers. For some customers, the focus on higher quality may mean greater order accuracy. For other firms it might mean on-time delivery schedules. For still others it means that the transaction is physically easy because, for example, the supplier offers EDI. Other firms want a knowledge transfer to accompany their tangible product purchase.

The vast majority of consulting firm clients, for example, now expect a relationship rather than a series of projects. They ask for a knowledge transfer or a facilitation process. It is no longer acceptable for consultants to just hand over expert judgments.

Another example can be found in the advertising world, where it is no longer acceptable to just turn over good creative work to win or keep an account. Media planning is becoming unbundled, and buyers are trying to pay just for the creative element. Many companies take separate media planning and creative pitches from the same agency. For too long, many ad agencies thought that they could impose their ad agency world view on what their clients would buy. Consequently, the ad agency world has become fragmented, with large and small firms competing for the same large accounts.

A national fast-food franchise, for example, uses one unified message created by an ad agency, and national campaigns planned once a quarter. The bulk of the remaining advertising dollars is then divided between the large ad agency media department and any number of local media houses that have the support of the local franchisees in their area, all of whom have equal access to pricing information. A prime example of how buyers are reexamining their approach to multiple ad agency support was highlighted when IBM consolidated all of its ad agency work into one $500 million account with Ogilvy & Mather.

According to IBM, the rationale for such a move was simple: One agency can add more value by dint of gaining an in-depth understanding of IBM.

FACING THE NEW REALITY

The balance of power between customers and suppliers has shifted significantly toward the customer, and executives must accept the new realities of greater buyer power. There are three basic options available:

1. *New product offerings.* Gamble on regaining some of the power through a quantum shift in product technology or a price that redirects the power balance to the seller.
2. *Productivity improvement.* Increase productivity within the existing framework of less supplier power.
3. *Reengineering.* Find ways to engage customers in a totally new kind of relationship. Anticipate and execute against customer needs from sales and service processes so well that customers line up to share their power.

The first option is not viable for most firms because few companies enjoy product advantages or have the opportunity to establish them. The second option, increasing sales productivity, has eluded even the best efforts of many top companies. The third option for dealing with the realities of new customer power—reengineering for a new kind of relationship—is the most viable option for most companies and the focus of this book. In fact, the first two options—product advantages and increased sales productivity—may best be pursued by engaging the customer in a relationship of enduring value, with all of the innovations and improvements that it entails, rather than continuing in an outmoded attempt to sell to customers.

C H A P T E R
T W O

THE NEW PROCUREMENT

The driving force of professional purchasing functions today is the desire for longer-lasting and closer relationships with fewer suppliers. Just as conglomerates are spinning off businesses that stray from their core competencies (for example, Kodak's sale of Sterling Drug), procurement departments are shrinking their sources of supply, and the rationale behind both trends is similar: to focus. Conglomerates are returning to their core competencies, and procurement departments are reaching into the inner realms of a smaller set of supplier organizations for customized product offerings and more added value.

A growing number of companies are realizing that reaching world-class status means achieving world-class procurement capability. This goal is propelling longer buyer/supplier relationships, a cross-functional approach to making procurement decisions, and direct procurement involvement in suppliers' design, manufacturing, and logistical supply functions. Firms that have consolidated their supply bases have discovered the cost savings and quality improvements that are possible when the relationship between purchaser and supplier is restructured for their competitive advantage.

The new reality in dealing with customers is that they have more power than ever before. This chapter outlines how suppliers can begin to redress the balance of power between buyers and suppliers. Suppliers can do this by reengineering their sales and service processes to better anticipate and execute against customer needs. A critical first step in this direction is developing a clearer picture of procurement today.

PRESSURES ON THE PROCUREMENT FUNCTION

In the same way that executives face new external and internal pressures to build their sales forces as platforms for competitive advantage, procurement agents now face pressures to create competitive advantage through strategic purchasing. According to the Center for Advanced Purchasing Studies (CAPS, 1993), the cost of production-related goods and services averages 60 percent of sales and runs as high as 85 percent of sales in certain industries, such as consumer electronics. In the automotive and electronics industries, payments to suppliers account for 60 to 70 percent of costs. Purchasers are acting to cut costs by up to 30 percent and to boost quality by closely managing their suppliers.

CAPS also conducted a recent survey of *Fortune* 500 CEOs and presidents and found that these executives expect the purchasing function to provide major input on material quality management and international sourcing. Three-quarters of the CEOs and presidents expect it to improve or maintain material quality, and almost 90 percent expect purchasing to assure external customer satisfaction. A full 70 percent expect purchasing to develop partnerships with suppliers.

These executives believe that purchasing can have an impact on quality, customer satisfaction, profitability, and market share. Their firms set purchasing goals and strategies that support the overall business plan. Two-thirds believe that purchasing's primary impact is on the firm's bottom-line profits; more than half believe that purchasing has a major impact on production and operations. They believe that the internal organization must be educated about the strengths and weaknesses of its supply base.

They also believe that the effectiveness of the information and communication system between buyers and suppliers is critical.

PROCUREMENT TRENDS

A 1993 CAPS survey of purchasing officers identified the following top 10 trends in purchasing:

1. Fewer sources of supply will be used.
2. Purchasers will be more concerned with final customer satisfaction.
3. Purchasers will manage supplier relations.
4. Purchasers will drive shorter cycle times.
5. Supply chain management will receive greater emphasis.
6. Design engineers and buyers will be part of sourcing teams.
7. Global sourcing will increase.
8. Order releasing will be relegated to users.
9. Teams will make sourcing decisions.
10. Single-sourcing will increase.

These trends reflect the new power and proactivity of the procurement function and the drive for more thorough management of a firm's suppliers. In fact, the surveyed purchasing officers predicted that purchasing will not be called "purchasing" by the year 2000, but will be known in its new proactive state as *supply management* or *sourcing management*.

The same survey found a strong trend toward building commodity teams or cross-functional sourcing teams, consisting of representatives from design, manufacturing, finance, marketing, quality, and purchasing. A 1990 Michigan State University study found that almost 80 percent of the surveyed firms plan to emphasize the use of cross-functional teams to support procurement and sourcing decisions over the next three years. Another central procurement trend is the increase in partnering arrangements and multiyear contracts. Procurement agents are clearly moving away from traditional bid-buy market operations and toward long-term relationships. All of these trends indicate that suppliers will have to change not only what they supply, but how they supply it.

FEWER SUPPLIERS

The single most important trend in procurement today is the rapid shrinking of the supplier base. The decline in the average number of suppliers per procurement category has averaged 8 percent per year over the past five years (CAPS, 1993). Companies involved in consolidating their supplier base commonly cut the base in half over a period of a few years. Some companies have reduced their supplier base by 90 percent. Increasingly, the purchasing function will consist of fewer people managing fewer suppliers, with an emphasis on end-user satisfaction. According to John Emswiller (*The Wall Street Journal*, August 16, 1991), Motorola, for example, has reduced its 10,000-company supplier base by more than 70 percent. Xerox has reduced its supplier base from 5000 to about 500 over the past decade.

SINGLE-SOURCING

The growth of aggressive supply management is closely tied to the equally dramatic growth of single-sourcing. Single-sourcing is a major trend in procurement. One of the greatest benefits of single-sourcing for procurement is that it allows for closer and more efficient supplier management. Single-sourcing also simplifies the just-in-time supply arrangements that are increasingly popular in manufacturing.

Many companies are outsourcing all nonstrategic components and services that are outside the core competencies of the firm. Manufacturing firms are using single-sourcing for an average of 35 percent of all their supplies. Nonmanufacturing firms use single-sourcing for an average of 30 percent of their needs. There is a higher incidence of single-sourcing among high-technology manufacturing industries than in nontechnical industries. Product quality is a critical success factor for these high-tech firms, and consistently high quality levels come from the constant stream of enhancements possible through single-sourcing with a quality supplier.

Single-sourcing can lead to long-term contracts and partnerships. It also enhances the broader trend toward supply chain management, with purchasers telling their suppliers who they want them (the suppliers) to buy from.

The amount of single-sourcing now found among manufacturing firms will eventually increase the trend toward single-sourcing in other sectors of the economy. The important point here is that there clearly is pressure for purchasers to use fewer suppliers for both services and tangible products. Reengineering can help companies ensure that they are ready when the purchasing departments of their large customers decide to use a single source. For example, if a supplier knows that a customer is putting more effort into reducing their overall procurement expenses, the supplier can position itself by demonstrating how its reengineered warehouse and logistical operations can lead to reduced purchasing costs.

CLOSER RELATIONSHIPS WITH LONGER TIME HORIZONS

Single-sourcing, multiyear contracts, and partnerships reflect the greater depth and much-expanded time horizons of modern buyer/supplier relationships. The amount of investment or risk that purchasers take when they shrink their supplier bases to only the most qualified means that, in turn, they expect that investment to pay off over time. The time horizon for the realization of significant cost savings and quality improvements through single-sourcing is about five years (CAPS, 1993). Partnerships survive an average of nine years—a considerable length of time in the new high-technology environment. Some companies make sourcing decisions even before the product design process begins. Suppliers may be signed on before the product design and development phases and may remain an integral part of the production process for the life of the product.

Longer time horizons are a significant shift from the purchasing patterns of the 1960s through the early 1980s. During those years, purchasing power was expressed as the ability to lower short-term prices. The favored technique for achieving this goal was to have five or six suppliers competing against each other to provide the best price. The quality movement's emphasis on fully evaluating the operational costs, efficiencies, and wealth creation capabilities of supplier products and services has replaced this old model of purchasing techniques, a model that was focused on lowering the initial purchase price. Instead, current procurement techniques focus on planning, measuring, and managing, with the intention of locking in the enduring value provided by a supplier relationship.

The desirability of longer time horizons also corresponds to the growing complexity of customer needs. For example, purchasers' evaluations of performance claims increasingly include multiyear supplier performance. This also applies to the services a customer buys from a professional services firm, such as a law firm, consulting firm, or accounting firm. When a customer buys professional services, they expect the advice acquired to move their organization forward for a long time.

The more the product offering is complex, customized, and consultative—whether tangible or intangible—the more likely that the time horizon for full evaluation will be longer. The purchaser and the supplier both need a longer amount of time to fully transfer the knowledge of what works for the client firm. Consequently, the customer's evaluation of the supplier and its products is provided and also accumulated over a relatively long time.

Some of the performance criteria that suppliers must meet may only come into play after a significant amount of time has passed—more than a single fiscal year, for example. The elongated time horizons captured in multiyear contracts or partnerships give suppliers the volume and confidence they need to make the investments necessary for raising quality and reducing the customer's true purchase and operating price/value concerns—the basis for considerable competitive advantage.

SUPPLY MANAGEMENT

Purchasers are also demanding closer attention from their suppliers through tighter performance management. Even though the first contact may come from the seller, who initiates the relationship by introducing their products or services, the action quickly moves from proactive prospecting to responding to customer evaluations. Proactivity may begin with the seller, but the power passes quickly to the customer. In the past, it was the supplier who had the power to initiate plus the power to disclose or withhold information about their products and the accuracy of their performance claims. Today, a tremendous amount of information is available to the customer, and many suppliers have lost the opportunity to use unsubstantiated performance claims.

The most common areas of customer involvement in the details of the supplier operations are through joint efforts to ensure continuous quality improvements and cost-reduction results. Firms commonly qualify suppliers to determine their present level of quality, then work with those suppliers for improvement, and, finally, certify them for dock-to-stock delivery.

Two dimensions of supply management are of particular relevance to suppliers: procurement's approach to supplier evaluation, and the impact of the quality movement on the customer/supplier interface.

SUPPLIER EVALUATION.   The customer's evaluation of a supplier hinges on three questions:

1. Does the supplier's product or service perform as claimed?

2. Will the supplier work with the customer to ensure continuous quality improvement?

3. Can the customer certify the supplier via performance evaluations? For some firms, determining whether a supplier can be certified may require constant evaluation over a year or more.

Answering the customer's first question often requires engineer-to-engineer contact—products offering specifications often require technical review. The second question can be answered only by evaluating senior executive or managerial commitment. The third question—can the supplier actually perform as agreed?—is evaluated over time, with a number of functional areas involved in the evaluation.

Procurement agents now demand information from the supplier on the supplier's costs, and they may demand justifications for certain costs. They may demand specific, ongoing quality improvements. Some purchasers demand that a cross-functional selection of the supplier's employees serve on intercompany product development and design teams. Other companies, such as Honda and Bose, have actually moved suppliers into offices at their companies. In some cases, supply management means chain management, and the purchaser may demand that specific suppliers be used.

QUALITY INTERFACE. Manufacturing firms that are deeply committed to the teachings of the quality movement have highly developed procedures for actively managing their relationships with suppliers. Their purchasing and manufacturing functions are more closely interfaced in the area of quality improvement than in any other area. Supplier involvement in a customer's manufacturing systems may include quality improvement or time-to-completion improvement programs, new product development projects, acquiring or jointly building new technology, and benchmarking projects.

In most cases, the focus is on short-term problem-solving activities—for example, improvements in product quality—

rather than on upstream integration through the product development cycle. The benefits a customer's procurement process now seeks through improved supply management include eliminating inspections of incoming materials and components and daily delivery of zero-defect parts to reduce inventory costs.

Purchasing activities and responsibilities traditionally include negotiations, determining price, where to buy, price analysis, and monitoring supplier quality. But a growing number of firms are reengineering their own cross-functional teams to make better sourcing decisions. These teams select suppliers, set target prices, and determine specifications and costs.

STRATEGIC SUPPLIER PARTNERING

Partnering is characterized by long-term commitments, information sharing, continuous improvement efforts, and the sharing of risks and rewards. Strategic partnerships allow a company to outsource critical components but still retain some measure of control over how the component is produced and sold.

The 1993 CAPS study of international strategic supplier partnerships concludes that successful partnering relationships develop slowly. Successful partnering depends on top management support, joint cross-functional teams, and a shared continuous improvement philosophy. The study notes that, as of 1992, strategic supplier partnerships (SSPs) commonly accounted for less than 1 percent of the supply base of *Fortune* 500 firms.

CAPS contrasts the cooperative-collaborative model of partnering with a competitive-coercive model that pits buyers and suppliers against each other in negotiations over price and the terms and conditions of the sale. Relationships within the competitive-coercive model are transaction-oriented, and switching suppliers often to get a lower price is common. Within the cooperative-collaborative model, the focus is on the total cost of the purchase and on mutually advantageous relations. Switching suppliers is rare and single-sourcing is common. In the most complete forms of partnerships or multiyear single-sourcing arrangements, the lines between the purchaser and the supplier blur, and suppliers are managed as an integrated part of the purchasing firm.

Procurement trends that have encouraged strategic supplier partnering include:

- Higher levels of quality consciousness
- Supplier involvement in design/redesign
- Emphasis on cycle-time reduction and speed to market
- Improved information technology
- Increases in firms' total costs of purchased materials, capital equipment, and services
- Reduction of supply bases
- Just-in-time philosophies

Strategic supplier partnering requires strong links among marketing, manufacturing, technology, financial, and human resource development strategies. Partnerships are usually oriented around the supply of direct material and are less prevalent for MRO, capital equipment, and services. These relationships take a long time to build and evolve. On average, companies using SSPs generally anticipate a relationship of 14 to 15 years, according to the CAPS study. Joint buyer/supplier multidiscipline teams push for continuous improvement across the full life cycle of the partnership.

Technical, quality, design, process, cost, and other confidential information is shared by both parties. SSPs are often the result of multiple successful interactions. The intent of the long-term commitment is to provide mutual benefit. Generally, a process for completing comprehensive supplier performance evaluations is already in place.

AN EXAMPLE OF THE NEW PROCUREMENT CAPABILITY

One of the most obvious and publicized examples of the new procurement approach is Wal-Mart. Wal-Mart expects some of its suppliers to put permanent sales and service teams in place. Procter & Gamble, for example, has an 80-person team in Bentonville, Arkansas, where Wal-Mart is based. Wal-Mart expects its vendors to be marketing partners—to do marketing research for Wal-Mart and give presentations on how best to sell their products through Wal-Mart. Wal-Mart's information system gives suppliers updates on sales by product and store every 90 minutes.

Wal-Mart also expects its vendors to follow certain distribution technologies. Procter & Gamble, for example, developed its distribution technology so that it meets Wal-Mart's needs. P&G backs up its trucks so that loaders walk the boxes across to Wal-Mart trucks. There is basically no warehousing. P&G has to comply to Wal-Mart's logistical operations, not the other way around.

When Wal-Mart told P&G that it wanted a whole P&G team to relocate to Bentonville, someone at P&G had to crunch those numbers to see how much P&G would have to increase its product prices to cover that cost. Real changes had to occur because P&G had to maintain its bottom-line profitability and stability while meeting Wal-Mart's requirements.

Of course, the supplier reaps real advantages. If a supplier has dominant share inside Wal-Mart, it knows that it has a certain amount of its capacity—20 percent, for example—already taken up. The supplier can then offer its product to other customers at very competitive prices because it has stabilized at least 20 percent of its business. In Wal-Mart's relationship with its large suppliers, Wal-Mart makes guarantees about the size of the shelf space that the suppliers will be given, and the switch-out costs are high.

BUYER/SUPPLIER RELATIONSHIPS ABROAD

The new procurement trends in the United States exist in much fuller form in Japan and Europe. Companies in Japan and Europe learned long ago that quality and cost management are best achieved by limiting the number of suppliers and working closely with them in long-term relationships geared to maximum competitive advantage for both parties. Buyer/supplier partnerships—the ultimate form of cooperation for joint competitive advantage—are now a major purchasing initiative in Europe and Asia.

A 1992 CAPS report on international buyer/supplier partnering found that partnerships are in place in a large cross section of industries throughout the world, and may become necessary for survival. The CAPS study notes that the partnership concept is well known in Europe, and that many European firms are pursuing partnerships with an emphasis on service-related and subcontracting arrangements. In Japan, partnerships are formed within *keiretsus*—corporate groupings with cross-ownership ties—and between independent companies.

EXAMPLES OF FUNCTIONING PARTNERSHIPS

The CAPS study includes the following examples of European and Japanese buyer/supplier arrangements:

- A German firm that manufactures power supply units and explosion-proof equipment works with a handful of customer-partners and does the same with its own suppliers who are, for the most part, single sources. Its partnering arrangements are covered by written contracts that last seven to eight years and are then commonly rolled over. Generally, cost savings are shared 50-50. The firm shares technological information as early as three to four years before it introduces a new product. It also provides its customers with detailed cost information on materials, labor, and overhead.

- A Japanese electronics manufacturer has partnership arrangements with about 120 of its suppliers. The buyer's purchasing function, staffed primarily with engineering and quality control employees, is the main point of contact with suppliers, but other functions are integrated into the purchasing process. The firm holds weekly meetings with its suppliers. Both parties exchange information on a number of topics, including costs and profit margins. Both parties also trade employees for extended stays to improve their understanding of each other's needs. If a supplier's performance drops below competitive standards, the buyer sends in a support team to help make the necessary improvements.

- A Scottish fabrication supplier offers a complete design/procure/manufacture/distribute service to its customers. It runs its own high-tech training center to refine its JIT (Just-In-Time), TQM (Total Quality Management), and cycle-time reduction techniques. The firm's sales force develops and maintains the buyer/supplier partnerships until the relationships are mature, and then hands them off to the firm's planning department, at which time they become the day-to-day interface with the customer. One six-year partnership with a customer has reduced the defect rate from 1.5 to 0.005 percent, increased on-time delivery from 97 to 100 percent, and shortened lead time from 40 to 10 days.

- A British employment agency supplies a manufacturer with its entire assembly work force and all related human resource management functions: hiring, evaluation, payroll, government reporting, and some training functions. The supplier maintains an on-site office and uses daily computer reports to monitor varying labor requirements. Monthly meetings between the buyer and supplier are used to evaluate supplier performance. The arrangement is covered by a three-year contract which will probably become evergreen.

- A Japanese automaker has 300 active suppliers, with an equity stake in about 20 of them. Outsourced parts account for 80 percent of its total direct costs. Joint buyer/supplier teams work during development and production, with suppliers involved from the inception of each new model. There are no written contracts. The buyer and its suppliers trade technical teams on an ongoing basis. Cost reduction goals are set jointly with each supplier.

The advantages of closer buyer/supplier relationships are so well accepted abroad that some European and Asian governments have developed government/industry initiatives to promote supplier development and buyer/supplier partnering. The British government, for example, sponsors a project called Partnership Sourcing, Ltd., to encourage British firms to form supplier partnerships.

THE JAPANESE MODEL

Unlike their European counterparts who first explored partnering in the 1980s, Japanese companies have used single-sourcing, or sole-sourcing, and partnerships with their suppliers for decades. Japanese buyers establish long and close relationships with their suppliers. Sole-sourcing is far more common in Japan than in Europe or the United States.

Japanese suppliers enter the production process at the earliest stages of design and often exchange engineers or form project teams with the customer's key employees. Suppliers share detailed cost information with buyers and work for relatively low profit margins. Their ongoing financial viability rests on their ability to continuously improve efficiency and productivity and to utilize economies of scale.

Buyers actively aid their suppliers in raising quality and lowering costs. Although new suppliers may be added to cover new technological requirements, it is uncommon for buyers to end a relationship with a supplier. Relationships with first-tier suppliers often span generations.

KEIRETSUS. A large number of close buyer/supplier relationships also exist within the context of Japanese keiretsus, the cooperative groups of companies organized around banks or trading companies to maximize competitive advantage and market share for the group as a whole and for each member individually. Buyers within the keiretsu commonly hold their suppliers to the highest standards for quality and price, but work extensively with their suppliers to ensure that they can meet the buyer's demands.

These suppliers then move into global markets in an advanced competitive position. The business group strategy, used in different forms in both Germany and Japan and a central force in their competitive success, is really an extended version of the buyer/supplier cooperation that characterizes the most advanced U.S. firms.

JAPANESE FIRMS IN THE UNITED STATES. The Japanese approach is spreading as the advantages of single-sourcing become apparent and as Japanese companies look for suppliers on a global basis and invest in companies abroad. Japanese firms operating in the United States generally bring their supply management model with them. At Japanese auto manufacturing plants in the United States, for example, U.S. suppliers are commonly required to beef up their research and design capabilities to meet Japanese expectations for suppliers to design and develop parts in-house.

Nissan sends its own engineers to examine prospective suppliers for its U.S. plants and helps suppliers redesign jobs for greater efficiency. In one case, Nissan's engineers more than doubled productivity at one parts supplier's plant. Nissan also offers training programs for suppliers' managers on topics ranging from problem solving to quality.

U.S. automakers are now shifting their supply management strategies to match the Japanese approach by increasing presourcing—in other words, by choosing suppliers before parts are designed. Chrysler presourced 95 percent of the parts for two of its recent new models, compared with 50 percent of the parts for models produced in its first attempt to use the Japanese approach. Chrysler also followed the Japanese style in stipulating long contracts lasting for at least the life of the model. These contracts contained incremental price reductions based on the assumption that buyer/supplier cooperation would improve efficiency and lower costs.

IMPLICATIONS FOR SUPPLIERS

The new procurement trends discussed in this chapter present suppliers with the serious implications listed in Figure 2-1. Most companies who take these trends and implications seriously conclude that their existing methods for sales and marketing must undergo a major revolution.

The next chapter provides a more detailed understanding of the procurement process, and then the remainder of this book addresses how companies need to respond to the challenge of growing procurement capabilities.

THE NEW PROCUREMENT: IMPLICATIONS FOR SUPPLIERS	
Procurement Trend	**Supplier Implication**
Fewer Suppliers	◆ Continued rationalization of weaker firms
	◆ Fewer bid opportunities
	◆ Greater emphasis on hit rate
Single-Sourcing	◆ Higher new-customer acquisition costs
	• More emphasis on selling cost control
	• Greater levels of selling sophistication required
	◆ Greater importance of existing customers
	• Increasing willingness to cut margins to maintain current customers
	• Heavier emphasis on monitoring customer satisfaction
Closer Relationships	◆ Greater customer access to supplier
	• Many functions interact with customer
	• Broader responsibility for meeting customer needs
	• More positions required to have customer contact skills and capabilities
	◆ Greater commitment to helping customers compete
Longer Time Horizons	◆ Annual measures give way to longer-term measures
	◆ Lower first-year profitability of new accounts
	◆ More sophisticated customer profitability planning
	◆ Emphasis on consistently meeting contractual obligations
	◆ Less viability of "loss-leader" pricing strategies
Supply Management	◆ More emphasis on joint assessment of supplier performance
Strategic Supplier Partnering	◆ More willingness to share sensitive financial information
	◆ Not a major issue for the immediate future; will be more of an outgrowth from other trends

Figure 2-1

MODELS OF PROCUREMENT

Understanding the procurement capability of a particular customer requires knowing their procurement strategy: where it is and where it is going in the future. In this chapter, we present a model of modern procurement which can help companies align their processes with their customers. We will also review traditional models of purchasing to highlight the degree to which this function has evolved in the last few years.

MODERN PROCUREMENT

A summary of a modern procurement process is provided in Figure 3-1. There are three primary sets of procurement processes: identification, specification, and exchange. While there is a logical flow from one set of processes to the next, they do not always follow in sequence. For example, simple rebuys may utilize only the specification process. Modified rebuys may require only slight changes in supplier assessment criteria and purchasing strategy. Following are more detailed descriptions of what occurs in each set of procurement processes.

IDENTIFICATION

During identification, customers review internal needs and conduct a preliminary scan of potential sources. By conducting both reviews simultaneously, buyers are able to establish a more refined sense of internal customer needs and the various criteria

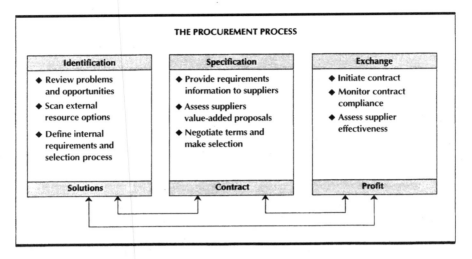

Figure 3-1

for evaluating how suppliers can meet these needs. In addition, the customers determine procedures and decisions for buying a particular product or service offering during this process.

ACTIVITIES. The primary activity during identification revolves around determining whether an *efficiency buy* or a *value buy* is required. An efficiency buy reflects the need for the same product at a lower price, faster delivery time, or different lot size. These are modifications to the customer's existing way of operating that will reduce costs or slightly increase operational efficiency. An efficiency solution can also involve reducing the costs of ownership by improving the administrative procedures for securing or using the product. Such improvements might include more efficient legal approval, order entry and processing, or shipping arrangements. A value buy entails providing significant improvements that ultimately impact the customer's product offering. Dimensions to a value buy include major reductions in unit cost, modification of product features that allow for increased profitability or market share, or operational process changes which significantly improve product quality or productivity.

During the identification stage, line managers, engineers, operators, and purchasing experts help their internal customers iteratively define their potential solutions in efficiency or value enhancement terms. For example, manufacturing personnel may think an efficiency solution is needed, but several value enhancement opportunities may offer greater gains. Or manufacturing personnel may assume that an enhancement solution is needed, when an efficiency solution could address most of their needs in a fraction of the time it would take to complete the value enhancements.

Buying skillfully is totally different in this new environment. Buying teams ensure that the business comes first, and functional perspectives second. The teams expect suppliers to think the same way and to interact in language that is adapted to the teams' particular business situation. Otherwise, the suppliers cannot assist them in the review.

In a newly identified opportunity, departments deeply embedded in the customer's firm, such as design, engineering, and manufacturing, commonly serve up the first set of definitions of their needs. In a rebuy situation, decision making is delegated to personnel in the more execution-oriented functions such as purchasing. Developing how and determining who has the responsibility for orchestrating the evaluations of supplier proposals and who has how much negotiating authority are established during this phase.

The information gathering in the first stage may be an entirely internal process or may include supplier-provided data and industry insights. Often it is not clear whether the customer or the supplier will be the proactive party who first identifies the opportunity. It may be that the customer is proactive in stating what it needs and in lining up suppliers to provide it. Or a supplier may approach a customer and show the customer solutions that the supplier believes the customer will find useful.

This first stage in the procurement process, then, is largely an information-gathering process: the interchange of data around the specifications, size, and scope of the opportunities and potential values to be exchanged between potential customers and potential suppliers. Even a traditional supplier going through rebuy reenters this stage as it puts together each proposal. As the decision makers within the customer organization reach agreement that there is a need for a broadly defined potential solution, the supplier begins to develop a selling approach to determine how the supplier can best specify the differentiation of its product offering to the customer as both move to a more formal stage of negotiations.

OUTCOME. The identification process ends with the adoption of the first definition of a potential solution. The process is usually very fluid up to the point where the potential solution is stipulated. Sometimes, this is expressed by an RFP (Request for Proposal), a requisition for supply, or instructions for the purchasing department to order. At that point, the process turns into internally formalized procedures and protocols. The customer has determined that there is a need for a solution and has started to specify the criteria for selecting a supplier.

SPECIFICATION

Once the potential solution is identified, the second part of the procurement process begins. In this stage, the customer defines and negotiates with suppliers for the value improvements the customer expects and the costs for those improvements.

ACTIVITIES. The customer presents its suppliers with its target solution, including design features, requirements for durability, terms, materials handling needs, quality standards, and logistical needs. It also describes the formalized process it will use for reviewing the suppliers' proposals. When the suppliers' presentations and responses are completed, the customer then selects a supplier. Very often, the customer attempts to negotiate additional terms—a lower final price or additional value, for example.

There may be a need for a stream of rebuying, where the supplier provides specific products or services at specific prices for a period of time or for an established purchase volume—a partnership or a sole-sourcing agreement, for example. Or the purchasing strategy might be to give the supplier 60 or 70 percent of the work, with the remainder going to another supplier in order to ensure a ready alternative or to negotiate a contract for a specified period of time. Or the purchasing strategy might be to use a certain supplier if the supplier agrees to purchase its materials from a particular source—in effect, managing the supplier's supply chain.

During specification, the customer assesses the value being proposed, either in terms of the customer's revenue enhancement potential, or in terms of a reduction in the customer's total supplier costs. Different buying influences within the customer's organization begin to articulate and review whether a supplier could be a partner, a sole source, a preferred source, a dominant share, or just another specified provider. The job of the supplier's sales force is to lock out the competition and to move as far up as desirable from an alternative supplier to a preferred provider to a sole-source contract, and finally, if appropriate, to a partnership.

The procurement process of many companies is now very open to considerable supplier involvement during specification. Customers realize that they can obtain much free consulting from potential suppliers. In fact, the value added during specification is taken as an indication of a supplier's overall capability to deliver on its promises.

More importantly, buyers now realize that the quality of the thinking surrounding specification can be more important than the product purchased. The degree to which the problem of the buyer's internal customer *is* solved, and the care taken to think through how the problem will *be* solved, can make as much of a difference as the features and benefits of the product being purchased. Buyers now expect much of today's competition among suppliers to occur on the consulting side of the specification process.

One of the consequences of allowing suppliers to actively participate in the specification process is circumvention.

Suppliers will try to change the rules of the game to gain an edge. Buyers are fully aware of this tendency, and they manage it in different ways. Some companies are strongly biased toward keeping all suppliers on even ground. These buyers attempt to maintain tight control of the specification process to make sure that an "apples-to-apples" comparison can be made. Other buyers want to maximize the quality of the consulting they receive from their suppliers. In these cases, buyers will take suggestions from suppliers on appropriate steps. They will even allow the procurement process to move back into the identification phase, or forward into exchange, if the supplier's rationale seems to support the wisdom of such a shift.

Each company and buying situation has a different set of specification assumptions. Suppliers need to understand them and then develop a strategy for dealing with them. The potential supplier's strategy needs to maximize the potential benefit to the customer, as well as the probability for winning a profitable contract.

OUTCOME.   By this point, the customer has reached a decision on who it will buy from, how it will buy, and under what conditions, and the supplier requests an official recording of the negotiated exchange in the form of a purchase order, contract, or letter of agreement. Regardless of the format, the outcome is a contract for fulfillment.

EXCHANGE

Companies have traditionally regarded the purchasing process as nearly complete when the contract is signed—product delivery and payment were the only remaining details. From the perspective of modern procurement, however, much remains to be done, as the following paragraphs describe.

ACTIVITIES.   During exchange, the customer and the supplier continue to reexamine the value equation of their ongoing exchange. The supplier follows through with the execution of the sale and attempts to consistently deliver the highest value at the lowest cost over time to maximize the profitability of its engagement with the customer. The supplier or the customer may decide that the supplier is adding more value than anticipated, or the customer may decide that it needs to renegotiate terms by returning to the identification stage of procurement.

At this point, the goal of exchange is to continuously manage the value from its supplier engagements. The customer evaluates whether the supplier fully meets the projected and anticipated value. The customer and the supplier monitor, make adjustments, and communicate back and forth about whether the supplier is living up to expectations. Figure 3-2 illustrates some of the many criteria which customers consider to assess the value a supplier provides. By suggesting or demanding improvements, customers clear any obstacles that prevent a smooth exchange.

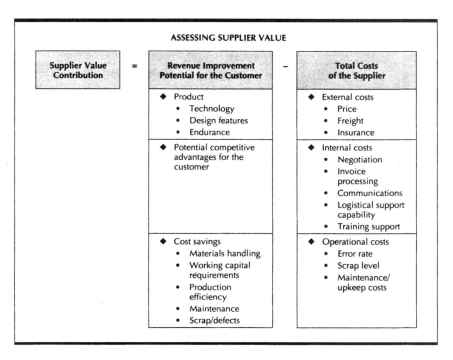

Figure 3-2

Customers assess the value of a supplier's total product offering by determining how much wealth creation will occur for them by dint of the overall product offering's technological features and quality. This calculation of revenue improvement potential considers the technology, design features, and zero-defect reliability of the product. Customers also determine the potential cost savings—materials handling, working capital requirements, production efficiencies, ongoing operational or maintenance costs, or the amount of scrap or defects, for example.

Formally or informally, the customer subtracts the total cost of the supplier's offering from its calculation of the offering's total value. The total cost of dealing with a particular supplier for a specific product includes external costs—the product price, freight, insurance—plus the customer's internal costs for using that supplier—negotiations, invoicing, communications, logistical capabilities, and training, for example.

During exchange, the purchase may be evaluated by the buyer, or by experts who evaluate specific technical requirements, or by the financial staff who evaluate the efficiency of the deal in hard dollars. Alternatively, the evaluation can be conducted jointly with the supplier. Often the final evaluation is communicated by the purchasing department, or, in the case of extremely valuable relationships, by the senior executives of the firm. The customer draws from these sometimes precise and sometimes approximate calculations during the exchange process, and concludes that either the engagement is profitable or it needs to be renegotiated back through the identification process.

OUTCOME.   The outcome of the exchange process encompasses the value of the entire procurement process. While purchasers can use the evaluation approach described in Figure 3-2, there is a long-term dimension to the relationship with suppliers. The outcomes that make for enduring and profitable relationships are satisfaction with the supplier, a match between the buyer's and the supplier's approaches to procurement, and the quality of the supplier's human resources that were assigned to work with the supplier. These "softer" dimensions, combined with assessments of value and profitability, make for enduring and profitable relationships.

LIVING IN THE MIDDLE

Although there is a dominant trend among many firms toward strategically upgrading purchasing capability, a wide range of procurement strategies exists. The range of procurement strategies spans two extremes. At one end of the spectrum, procurement agents still live in the old world of buying, where buyers maintain a relatively coercive relationship with a number of suppliers who compete primarily on the basis of price. At the other end of the spectrum, companies pursue strategic partnerships— that 1 percent of their company-supplier relationships that spans decades and blurs the lines between buyers and suppliers.

Most buyers and suppliers live somewhere in the middle and will continue to do so for the foreseeable future. The middle is where hard decisions must be made. The middle is where elements of the old model and elements of partnering combine to produce the buyer/supplier relationships that are most difficult to understand, depend on, or invest in wisely.

In the chaotic middle, there are many variations of buyer/supplier relationships. They may include contact between a purchasing agent and a salesperson, or between a cross-functional sourcing team and a cross-functional product design team. The common denominator is that the buyer decides what the configuration will be, based on the buyer's projected understanding of the total value likely to be added from the product offerings of competing suppliers. The information used to understand supplier performance claims ranges from the supplier's annual report to joint testing of a supplier's sources. Under any circumstances, the decision is the buyer's choice, whether it occurs at the buyer's or supplier's initiative.

In this middle realm, the customer may reach deep into the supplier's organization to link up with employees who can validate the proclaimed value or document the performance claims. The performance claims may include not only how the product performs but how the product will be delivered, serviced, and supported. The purchase may be contingent on the supplier meeting various product performance specifications, or guaranteeing locations or schedules, or the ease of communications provided by their EDI system.

Strategic partnering will grow where it can, but most companies are not in a position to use partnering exclusively, and some products are not suitable for partnering agreements. In strategic partnerships, the nature of the wealth creation is such that neither the purchaser nor the supplier needs to initiate specific requirements—the product itself drives the relationship between the buyer and supplier. Buyer/supplier relationships may take a variety of forms, but most stop short of the legal agreements and shared cost savings found in true partnerships. It is unlikely that strategic partnerships will ever become the dominant form of relations between purchasers and suppliers at this stage of economic development. But just selling the core product won't satisfy the customers most worth having. Unstable and unclear relationships in the middle range will dominate business-to-business transactions well into the next century. Under any circumstances, however, it is clear that customers are more proactive in their attempts to dominate the buyer/supplier relationship.

EXTERNAL AND INTERNAL SUPPLIER PROACTIVITY

Procurement functions are becoming more proactive. The trend cannot be reversed, but suppliers can recast their role and become proactive in terms of knowing the customers' needs, tracking the development of the customers' procurement capabilities, and forming mutually beneficial relationships with customers.

Purchasing is now demanding access to those decisions suppliers make that have a substantial impact on costs—make/buy and product design decisions, for example. But suppliers who face aggressive procurement agents need to respond in ways that benefit both the supplier and the customer. Suppliers may also need to develop their own proactive strategy to pull passive customers further along in their development.

The need for supplier proactivity comes from two directions. First, suppliers must come to understand their customers and provide them with substantive assistance in their quest for competitive status. For suppliers, most opportunities for proactivity will come from adding implicit services with economic value. Offering this kind of added value may make the difference for suppliers who need to lock out the competition. This proactivity in relations with customers is an external or outward-looking form of proactivity.

There is also a need for an internal form of proactivity: the proactivity of the customer coverage functions in their relations with other functions within the firm. Those who work in sales, marketing, or service functions must create a seamless interface with customers. Waiting for another function to take the initiative to pull the customer-facing functions together could take too long. Action is needed now.

The best place for a supplier to begin is to listen to its best and most demanding customers and assume that someday all its customers will reach the same level of skill and expectations. The key is to listen to those customers who have progressed most from their old purchasing methods and to watch how quickly other customers are reevaluating traditional methods and their purchasing agents.

TRADITIONAL PROCUREMENT MODELS

A variety of authors have described industrial and organizational buying behavior. Their models attempt to explain what makes customers buy. Some of these models are outlined in the next section of this chapter, including the buy-type, exchange, communications, and buyer segmentation models. While some customers have moved to the procurement model just described, others are still using older approaches to buying. These traditional models of buying are now reviewed.

BUY-TYPE MODEL

The model by Robinson, Faris, and Wind (1967, see Figure 3-3) examines three generic types of buying decisions: the new task, the modified rebuy, and the straight buy. These decisions are compared in terms of the degree of risk for the buyer, the amount of information required by the buyer, and the extent to which alternatives are assessed.

In this simple model, the most complex decision process involves the new-task buying situation. New buys occur less often than modified rebuys, which are the most common buying situation. Other researchers have proposed different buying situations and dimensions of difference, but the purpose is to categorize and describe different buying situations. It is our experi-

---

BUY-TYPE MODEL

Buying Situation	Degree of Buyer Risk	Information Requirements	Consideration of New Alternatives
New task	High	Medium	Important
Modified rebuy	Medium	Moderate	Limited
Straight rebuy	Low	Minimal	None

Source: P.J. Robinson, C. W. Faris, and Y. Wind, *Industrial Buying and Creative Marketing,* Allyn and Bacon, 1967.

Figure 3-3

ence that many buying and selling organizations have fully integrated buy-type thinking into their everyday selling and operating procedures.

EXCHANGE MODEL

Exchange models acknowledge that buying involves interchanges between and among parties. At the simplest level, an exchange is merely goods for payment. At more complicated levels, individual needs and contributions are examined in more detail, as can be seen in the model developed by Bonoma, Zaltman, and Johnston (1978, see Figure 3-4), depicting the primary exchanges among four groups at work in the buying and selling process.

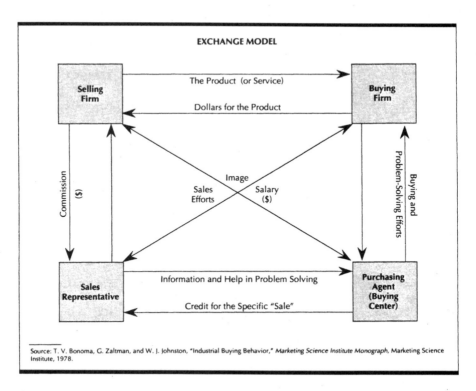

Source: T. V. Bonoma, G. Zaltman, and W. J. Johnston, "Industrial Buying Behavior," *Marketing Science Institute Monograph,* Marketing Science Institute, 1978.

Figure 3-4

The difficulty with exchange models is that the actual exchange varies dramatically by buy-type, and even from customer to customer. Again, an awareness of the exchange dimension to buying and selling interactions is well understood by today's sales forces.

COMMUNICATIONS MODEL

Johnston (1981, see Figure 3-5) developed a model hypothesizing that the likelihood of a purchase increases as lateral influ-

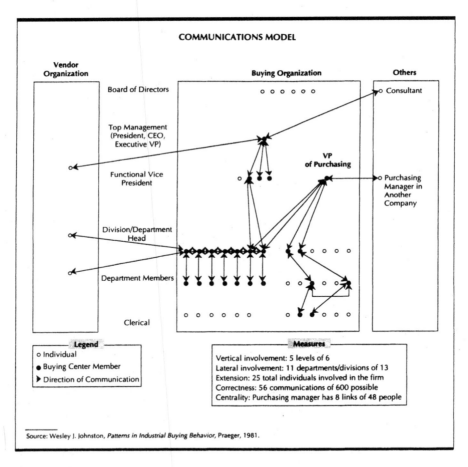

Figure 3-5

ence (across functions or departments) and vertical influence (from lower to higher levels of management) increase. Such models have led to many adaptations in modern selling, including the *strategic selling* approach by Miller (1989). Sales approaches geared to the communications model attempt to map out the decision-making process within the buying center, assess its impact on the sale, and then focus on developing account-specific selling strategies for winning the sale.

BUYER SEGMENTATION MODEL

Despite the fact that the sales function reports to marketing in many companies, there is an astonishing lack of market segmentation of customer sales and service preferences. Indeed, this major opportunity for marketing to add value to the sales function is typically overlooked. This gap was noted by Moriarty (1983, see Figure 3-6), who proposed applying traditional consumer market segmentation methods to customer buying factors. He examined a variety of buying factors across industry and

BUYING FACTORS
Importance of Product Attributes by Industry-Sector and Company-Size Segments
(Index of Ratings)

	Business Services (number of employees)			Wholesale/Retail (number of employees)			Finance (number of employees)			Manufacturing (number of employees)		
	<250	250 to 1,000	>1,000	<250	250 to 1,000	>1,000	<250	250 to 1,000	>1,000	<250	250 to 1,000	>1,000
Buying Factor					Number of Respondents							
	8	29	30	7	16	39	17	33	74	5	9	30
Speed	1.14	1.16	0.95	1.06	1.09	0.98	0.90	0.98	0.95	1.15	1.23	0.94
Operator	1.05	1.00	1.04	1.03	1.04	0.93	1.03	1.01	1.01	1.12	1.04	0.91
Aesthetics	1.07	1.01	0.99	0.99	1.02	0.96	0.81	0.97	1.10	0.88	0.93	0.94
Compatibility	0.93	1.02	0.94	1.04	1.03	1.01	1.05	1.03	0.99	1.01	1.18	0.94
Service	1.03	0.96	0.98	0.96	1.00	1.02	1.02	0.98	1.01	1.04	0.87	1.05
Delivery	0.88	0.96	1.01	1.08	1.05	1.02	0.94	0.98	1.01	0.81	1.07	1.05
Absolute Price	0.89	1.01	1.04	1.01	0.88	1.03	0.88	1.00	0.97	0.86	1.25	1.07
Price Flexibility	0.87	1.00	0.96	1.11	0.95	1.02	0.97	0.99	1.04	0.89	0.99	1.12
Software	1.01	1.00	1.07	1.04	0.94	0.98	1.14	1.06	0.96	0.95	0.94	0.97
Broad Line	1.02	1.16	0.95	1.10	0.92	1.07	1.05	0.96	0.94	1.23	0.82	1.03
Visibility Among Top Management	1.12	0.96	1.01	1.17	1.06	1.09	0.94	0.91	1.01	0.99	0.94	0.99
Manufacturer Stability	0.96	0.97	0.98	0.96	0.96	1.05	0.80	0.99	1.07	0.97	0.96	1.02
Sales Competence	1.12	0.97	0.96	0.95	1.13	0.95	1.09	1.06	0.91	1.10	1.14	0.96
Reliability	1.09	0.94	1.09	1.04	1.04	0.94	1.01	0.97	0.97	0.96	0.99	1.05

Source: Rowland T. Moriarty, *Industrial Buying Behavior*, Lexington Books, 1983.

Figure 3-6

company size categories, and examined how buyers in these industries differed on the emphasis they placed on the buying factors.

It could be argued that many companies have engaged in buyer segmentation, given the broad usage of national, key, and regional account designations, or A, B, C account classifications, which are used in many sales organizations. These approaches to segmentation, however, emphasize the supplier's need to maximize sales force productivity, not customer buying factors. On the other hand, the growing use of industry specialists is evidence that sales forces are beginning to acknowledge different customer need segments with organizational arrangements that align with true customer buying factors.

Suppliers can use the models described here to identify and think about where their customers are in their procurement development. This is the first building block in constructing a strategy for engaging customers in the twenty-first century. It offers a way to enhance communications between suppliers and customers when customers express their procurement objectives.

Until suppliers understand how quickly and thoroughly their customers are reengineering their procurement processes, they cannot redress the balance of power that now favors buyers. Reengineering the supplier organization to change this situation is the subject of the next several chapters. As the next chapter describes, many suppliers' processes for paralleling a customer's procurement process are flawed by a reliance on a series of outmoded concepts about value added. We provide alternative methods for determining how to continuously enhance the value of product offerings to the customer's wealth creation processes in ways that differentiate the supplier from the competition—all the way to a mutually profitable engagement.

LOOKING
INSIDE

Dramatic improvements in procurement capability offer suppliers tremendous strategic opportunities. To take advantage of the opportunity, a company must first appraise the effectiveness of its sales and marketing functions, and question the assumptions under which these functions have operated for decades. Second, a company should move to reestablish competitive advantage by meeting customers where they are, today and in the future. This section of the book draws heavily on the successes of leading firms to illustrate how strategies can be formulated to yield enduring and profitable customer relationships.

Chapter	Summary
4 Functions Are Failing	Traditional sales and marketing functions are in trouble. Buyers have taken the upper hand in selling, and they have changed the rules of marketing. In the past, sales and marketing were oriented toward attracting customers to the company; now competitiveness entails bringing the full resources of the company to the customer.
5 Enter the Engagement Era	The old terms of sales and marketing are outdated, and a new era of engagement has arrived. We use the term *engagement* to capture the process of bringing the company to the customer and interacting with the customer's procurement process. This chapter provides a summary of the engagement process, and introduces a strategic model for examining the financial contribution of the engagement process.

(Continued)

6 Disconnects and Potential	Is your company trapped in a bygone era of selling and marketing? What are the signs that your company has not adjusted to the new realities of modern procurement? What is the full range of value that can be added during the engagement process? These questions are answered by examining best practices across a variety of companies and industries.
7 Engagement Strategy	This chapter dives into the details of developing a comprehensive engagement strategy. Frameworks are provided that will help companies develop the means to: ● Define their competitive position throughout the engagement process. ● Assess how well they are achieving their target competitive position with customers. ● Identify engagement strategies that provide and sustain competitive advantage.

FUNCTIONS
ARE FAILING

In companies across North America, the sales and marketing functions are having serious trouble meeting the challenges customers present. Many sales and marketing executives are ignoring information about their declining effectiveness and are holding on to old methods for reaching and meeting customer needs. These two functions are not the major players they once were in many companies. In the foreseeable future, they are likely to be replaced with something different. Understanding the cause of this trend, and dealing effectively with it, requires a hard look at the internal forces that have led to this situation and have blocked constructive change. This chapter describes the declining effectiveness of sales and marketing functions in today's leading businesses, and the obstacles to creating the vision needed for meaningful change.

THE SALES FUNCTION

For at least the first half of this century, direct sales stood at the center of many organizations. The sales force was the primary means for reaching the customer and for bringing information about the customer back to the firm.

For the last several decades, however, the sales force has been in a defensive posture. Now sales managers must see the elements of truth contained within the attacks on sales—attacks which escalated rapidly as the teachings of the quality movement took hold. Sales managers must submit to a full self-evaluation. This means looking beyond data points to trends, and beyond the day-to-day grind of meeting immediate financial goals to the future of the sales function itself and its role within the company. The days of refusing to lead or participate in change efforts by raising the specter of adverse impacts on sales volume are over.

HOLDING THE COMPANY HOSTAGE

Some companies have been held hostage by the sales function for decades. While top executives might recognize the need for change, they have acquiesced to ominous sales management predictions that salespeople will leave for the competition and take their customers with them, or that orders will "disappear" and sales volume will decline.

Many sales executives know or have heard of companies that dared to change sales compensation or account assignments or restructure sales jobs, and consequently suffered devastating declines in sales productivity. In legal publishing, competitors tell the story of Matthew Bender's 1993 woes. Bender converted their sales force into a service organization, and inadvertently accelerated their decline in new sales volume. In automobile insurance, competitors point to AAA of Southern California, which changed its sales compensation program in the early 1990s, had poor results, changed it again, and ended up with a series of futile and costly attempts to redirect its sales force.

Virtually every industry has its examples of bold companies that tried to change their sales functions and suffered dire consequences. Sales executives tell these stories vividly to send the message that messing with sales is playing with fire. They caution that any radical change in the sales force may mean a decline in sales and consequent trouble with stockholders.

Sales forces have often been effective at issuing such warnings and exploiting management's fear of losing customers or sales volume. Top management has unwittingly induced this behavior in sales forces. Salespeople were encouraged to "own" their customers, and taught to think of their accounts as personal property, their territories as private hunting preserves. But "owning the customer" has become a double-edged sword. While clear accountabilities for sales were established, the practice kept other functions out of the sales process and gave companies an unhealthy dependence on a single function.

It is difficult for management to measure the validity of the claim of salespeople who say they can take their customers with them. Companies cannot accurately judge the customer's commitment to the company versus the commitment to the individual salesperson. It is hard to gather reliable information on customer loyalties and, frequently, no one besides the salesperson knows the customer personally.

It is also difficult to assess sales management's warnings of falling sales when suggestions are made to restructure or redirect the sales force. Top management frequently has not spent enough time in sales or with customers to judge for itself whether the doom and gloom forecasted by sales executives is warranted or can be avoided. Moreover, sales forces intensify their warnings as customer problems mount. But, at some point, management must not only heed, but look beyond, the warnings—especially when sales results continue to fall short.

Visible Damage

After years of accepting, if not perpetuating, this hostage situation, why is management beginning to draw the line with sales, call a halt, and objectively assess the value added by sales? In the good old days—the fifties, the sixties, the seventies—salespeople often were the heroes in the organization: the people who had the power to pull the company out of a slump or to beat back the competition with a superior sales effort. But over the past 15 or so years, the sales function has been less able to save companies from the grips of unprecedented international competition. Repeatedly, the sales force has promised a resurgence, only to return with a host of excuses at the end of the year: sales goals were too high, products and prices were uncompetitive, quality was too low, delivery and service were unacceptable, and so on. While the sales force blames other functions, top management eventually reaches the conclusion that, regardless of where the blame lies, this can't go on any more. Companies can't continue to hope that the sales force will go out next year and turn things around—it just isn't happening.

Too many well-known companies have relied heavily on their sales forces and have not been able to sustain their competitive position. At IBM, especially during the decade Buck Rodgers was vice president of marketing (refer to *The IBM Way* by Rodgers, 1986), sales was one of the most powerful and trusted functions in the company. When pressure first mounted for IBM to restructure while retaining its lifelong employment tradition, its first move was to shift people from plant and staff positions into sales. The idea was that this would be better for the customer and the company. But, as we all know now, sales was not the way out for IBM. In another highly publicized case, E. F. Hutton poured money into sales compensation to keep its powerful and widely admired sales force happy, and eventually bankrupted the company. Rather than being its most valuable asset, E. F. Hutton's sales force was its final undoing.

Myth of Lots of Data

Sales functions traditionally claim that they can produce a great deal of data on sales performance and that sales is the most highly quantified function in the firm. Sales is the only function, sales managers argue, that can actually claim responsibility for a line on the firm's income statement. Sales can track results by order, by customer, by territory, by product, by month or year-to-date, by this year versus last year, or by dollars versus units, by whatever you prefer. Impressive, right?

Maybe not. When forced to scrutinize sales performance more closely, management has discovered major information gaps on the cost impact of the sales function. For example, sales forces frequently do not know how their direct cost of sales compares to that of competitors. And what about other costs, such as discounts, promotional allowances, transportation? Then there are indirect costs surrounding sales errors such as incomplete or incorrect orders, and associated costs of wasted time, scrap, or the cost of rework. Shouldn't these be tracked?

Finally, there is price, cost of goods sold by standard or actual cost, customer profitability, customer satisfaction, internal customer satisfaction, employee satisfaction, and customer retention. Most sales forces do not have good information on these critical topics. Sometimes they argue that these measures are not their responsibility, that they don't control these variables.

Management cannot afford to buy this argument anymore. Management is starting to conclude that if you are going to take responsibility for customers, you have to take all of the responsibility. It just does not work to focus on the top line of the income statement and expect the rest of the company to take care of the rest. Too much of what happens below the gross sales line is driven by interactions with customers. Taking responsibility starts with getting the numbers. And right now, they don't exist in many companies. So, the claim that sales has the best information on performance needs to be reassessed.

RISING SELLING COSTS

The limited data that exists on the sales function often reinforces the belief that there is trouble in the sales force. Sales executives are under constant pressure to meet sales goals while cutting costs and increasing productivity. According to a Dartnel survey (as reported in *Sales & Marketing Management* by O'Connell in 1989), the actual cost of a business-to-business sales call rose at an annualized rate of just over 11 percent per year from 1977 to 1987. National account managers' sales calls run $500 per hour. These are embedded costs: part compensation and part technology, part office space and support, part benefits, and part perquisites. Few companies have succeeded in trimming cost per salesperson while maintaining the same level of effectiveness. Companies cannot raise product prices by 10 or 11 percent to cover these increasing costs. Over the same period, the average annual sales volume per salesperson has grown by a nominal rate of 5.5 percent. While the overall increase in the Producer Price Index has helped relieve the pressure of selling costs that were using faster-than-average sales volume, without the support of increased inflation, that relief does not add up to much.

One way to close the gap between rising selling costs and lower price increases is to focus on the numerator of the productivity equation (outputs divided by inputs) and increase sales per salesperson. Companies can counteract the increase in costs by using technology or support functions like telemarketing or customer service to leverage the salesperson's time so that he or she can spend more time actually *selling*, leading to higher sales per person.

The silver lining in this cloud is that the average *Fortune* 1000 company can make up for an 11 percent increase in selling expenses by increasing sales per person by less than 1 percent. But it's tough to increase sales per salesperson when the average salesperson only spends a third or less of his or her time actually selling. Management is always dismayed to discover that two-thirds of the average salesperson's time is spent chasing down orders, negotiating with management on customer requirements, completing paperwork, and performing other nonselling tasks. The proportion of the time spent with the customer must increase if organizations are to cope with rising selling costs—a key challenge for many reengineering efforts.

THE IMPACT OF THE QUALITY MOVEMENT

With all that management has learned from the quality movement over the past decade, warnings of trouble from sales are

and salespeople. The rationale was: "Lawyers like to argue, so you have to be ready to fence with them." Salespeople had always used pressure selling tactics to close the sale. They argued that if they did not close the sale when they were there in front of the customer, they would not have another chance, because they traveled from city to city and might not return for some time. By the time they were back in town, the customer might have bought the product from someone else.

Meanwhile, in its attempt to fight declining sales and find cheaper, more cost-effective means of distributing products, one publishing company discovered that its traditional face-to-face sales channel was growing more slowly than new channels such as telemarketing and direct mail. When it asked customers about their preferences and attitudes toward direct sales versus telemarketing, customers reported that they preferred telemarketing because they had more control over the situation on the phone; they could always hang up if they did not like the salesperson or the pressure exerted. Phone calls took less time and could be scheduled for their convenience. They felt they could just ask the salesperson to call back if they were busy.

IMPLICATIONS. These two examples—auto dealers and a legal publishing company—illustrate what many companies are discovering: Customers don't feel that salespeople are meeting their needs. Customers don't like being duped or told what to buy and when to buy it. They don't like salespeople calling on them without appointments or at the convenience of the salesperson. They don't like a train of different salespeople representing different products from the same supplier taking up their time. And they don't like salespeople asking them to wade through generic catalogs that don't provide information specific to their industry and their needs.

Ultimately, the sales function must change to meet the needs of the customer—to respond to the new procurement—or the customer will make the sales function obsolete and irrelevant and put it right out of business.

THE MARKETING FUNCTION

Despite its central role in many organizations, sales has been maligned from both inside and outside the company, and many have argued that sales should be subordinated to the marketing function. In an influential 1991 *Harvard Business Review* article called "Marketing Is Everything," Regis McKenna described selling as the process of tricking people into buying something. He implied that all salespeople are like Harold Hill in Meredith Willson's *The Music Man* or the salesmen in Barry Levinson's *Tin Men*. Philip Kotler (*Marketing Management*, 1988) adopts a similar position:

> The [selling] concept assumes that consumers typically show buying inertia or resistance and have to be coaxed into buying more...

The same is true for Peter Drucker (*Management: Tasks, Responsibilities, Practices*, 1973):

> There will always, one can assume, be need for some selling. But the aim of marketing is to make selling superfluous.

The need to move beyond traditional sales tactics has also been acknowledged from the sales side of the fence. Mack Hanan introduced *Consultative Selling* back in 1970. IBM used the concept of value-added selling long before Buck Rodgers wrote *The IBM Way* in 1986. For decades, R. R. Donnelley's salespeople have been widely respected in the printing industry as excellent business people who also know a lot about printing.

Despite these exceptions, the sales function has tended to view customers as having one set of needs: those that were addressed by their products. The beauty of marketing was that it added segmentation to the sales idea of the undifferentiated customer. With the explosion of alternative channels to communicate with customers and a proliferation of ways to buy, marketing could make selling more efficient. It could create additional demand for products through more efficient means than pounding the pavement or cold-calling for leads. The sales force had been the primary way to send messages to the customer, but with the advent of radio, television, and new inexpensive direct-mail technologies, companies could look to marketing in addition to sales to get the message out.

It was not that long ago that companies would note with pride in their annual reports that they were "marketing-driven." This would indicate to stockholders that the company had restructured to emphasize marketing and had adopted the latest management techniques. The marketing concept was an improvement on the sales concept. It helped companies better manage the profitability of their products by better predicting how groups of customers would respond to a product and how much of a product could be sold at a given price.

Marketing ended the days when sales too often moved the company to manufacture products with limited profitability. Marketing embraced a product profitability perspective and added a much needed boost of discipline and rigor to the process of identifying new product opportunities, enhancing product features, setting product price levels, selecting channels of distribution, and developing advertising campaigns. Companies were able to demonstrate quick and sure profit improvement opportunities by applying marketing science to the tangled web of products and customers created by the sales function.

Based on the financial impact marketers had on their companies, many quickly rose to top positions in corporate America. Marketers were the best and the latest of the new breed of professional managers. Frequently, CEOs were groomed by moving through the marketing hierarchy. Through this career path, these future CEOs worked closely with a number of other key functions and were well-versed in how they operated.

POOR FINANCIAL RESULTS

So what happened? How could marketing topple so quickly from its lofty leadership position? Even Kotler sees trouble on the horizon for marketing. At the Fourth Annual Global Conference on Marketing, Kotler acknowledged: "This is a critical time in marketing....Many of us will be obsolete" (as reported in the September 1994 issue of *Management Review*). For one, the financial results that were reaped in the sixties and seventies vanished for many companies in the eighties. Foreign competition was ruthless. No amount of marketing magic could avert the declines that were being suffered. There simply was too much overhead in corporate America, and manufacturing costs had to be slashed.

PERFORMANCE CLAIMS

Marketing and sales historically made performance claims that customers were unable to evaluate because they did not have access to the necessary information. Now, customers know as much, if not more, than marketers do about the true performance and operating costs of products. The quality movement forced a new analysis of the real value of the product offering—both acquisition and operational costs—so that customers now have a much better understanding of value delivered by a supplier.

The same developments known as *consumer power* in the consumer products arena are growing in business-to-business selling. If a consumer wants to buy a car, he or she may read *Consumer Reports* for evaluations of the various products and then go on-line on the home computer for further comparisons of product offerings and prices and to actually make the purchase. Investors can monitor their mutual funds in the same way. The same holds true for business-to-business selling. Buyers now have instantaneous access to inventory levels and turns or product performance characteristics. The key point is that customers have their own independent sources of information about product performance and no longer rely on marketing for that information. If knowledge is power, consumers have become very powerful. This buyer power is the centerpiece of the new procurement at the business-to-business level.

Big buyers have more power to enforce compliance with their rules, but both big and small buyers have access to the information that allows them to function without depending on the supplier to make and validate performance claims.

Marketers used to be able to focus on performance claims; now they can't. Marketing can no longer think in terms of push/pull, or setting the marketing mix purely in terms of its own interests. Segmentation of customers by performance claim worked 10 and 20 years ago, but it doesn't work today. Companies already know how well the product performs. Now suppliers are expected to provide solutions to problems, not just products. And this happens through relationships, by working with one customer at a time.

THE MARKETING MIX

Determining the marketing mix was once the sole purview of the supplier's marketing function. But in the customer-driven era, the new power of buyers includes the power to influence and, in some cases, actually dictate the marketing mix that the supplier will adopt.

In the grocery trade, for example, variables in the marketing mix include advertising, shelving allowances, promotions, and couponing. Suppliers traditionally have put money into promotions to stimulate growth. Shelving allowances occurred only when there was a new product. The supplier's goal was to get to the point where advertising dominated the mix because it was less expensive than couponing, promotions, or allowances. In marketing terms, pull is cheaper than push.

Now, stores have optical character recognition and the trade has learned much more about costs. Supermarket chains, hypermarkets, and department stores are reaching the Wal-Mart level of sophistication, where suppliers meet with procurement people who have current, complete data on all the products Wal-Mart sells. Wal-Mart instructs its suppliers on what merchandising and inventory work the suppliers must provide, and demands that the products sell for an everyday low price. It also insists that the suppliers provide coupons for Wal-Mart customers alone so that the store draws in more people and makes more money. And Wal-Mart commonly determines what type of couponing the suppliers should provide.

Increasingly, buyers are asking suppliers to do their marketing for them. They are insisting that suppliers own the inventory until it moves off the shelves. They pay suppliers after the product passes the cash register, not before—a complete reversal in cash flow. They are pushing a whole group of tasks and costs back onto suppliers.

In response to greater and greater distribution costs, suppliers are cutting their own suppliers, and putting the squeeze on them. One leading consumer food manufacturer, for example, had 8000 suppliers six years ago; today it has 2200. Suppliers are also cutting their work forces and trimming their costs wherever they can.

This process is most highly developed in the consumer products industry because much product performance data is available there, and buyers have become large and powerful. There is more information about total costs from gate to out the cash register. The profit economics of that industry are more clearly understood, shelf by shelf and product by product. Now, suppliers have to play by the buyers' rules.

But buyer influence on the marketing mix is also evolving in industrial sectors as well. The demand for solutions ultimately dictates what types of support services—installation and training, for example—are provided. And customers are forcing their suppliers to tailor these aspects of the industrial marketing mix to meet their unique needs as well.

Marketing still believes that the answer lies in interfacing through marketing tools—advertising, promotions, channel decisions, product features, product technology, price—but that is no longer the relevant arena. Buyers are demanding that suppliers change the product offering to include tailoring of the marketing mix to meet the buyer's unique requirements. Buyers have announced that it is their game. This may mean that the supplier's goal of increasing advertising and decreasing shelving allowances may be reversed by buyers who prefer to see marketing dollars directed to shelving allowances, newspaper circulars, or couponing.

THE QUALITY MOVEMENT

Marketing and sales lost their dominion over customers when the quality movement came to the forefront. In the past, manufacturing was cut off from the customer by sales and marketing. Most of what manufacturing knew about the customer was what they were told by these two functions. Now, quality and reengineering efforts initiated by manufacturing were bypassing sales and marketing, going straight to the customer, and finding that the picture was more complicated and quite different from the one painted by marketing and sales.

By going directly to the customer, manufacturing found that more than a quality product was needed to meet customer needs. A wide variety of processes needed to be coordinated to satisfy a wide spectrum of customer requirements involving specification, delivery, installation, training, assessment, respecification, and so on in a continuous cycle of improvement. These first-generation reengineering and quality initiatives made it clear that the customer needed things that were not being provided by the company, that manufacturing alone could not provide them, and, that neither marketing nor sales really had a complete grasp of customer needs.

FUNDAMENTAL FLAWS

As manufacturing drove to match the competitive quality levels of international rivals, it discovered that sales and marketing were falling short in their role of relaying customer needs to the company. This was an indication that there were fundamental flaws in the marketing concept. How else could such a gaping hole have opened during marketing's watch over customer needs?

Much of the answer to this question rests in reexamining the fundamental assumptions and precepts of the marketing concept. In many ways, marketing means *bringing the customer to the company*. But today's economic climate requires *bringing the company to the customer*. The marketing concept falls short in that it does not address the customer's needs for tailored solutions or intensive support after the sale. Today, enduring success involves much more than delivering a product that has the features the customer needs at a competitive price. Product and price are assumed as minimum requirements by customers; it's how the offer is tailored and delivered that counts.

Evidence of "pull" marketing limits can be found in advertising and promotion trends. For one, these expense items are declining as a percent of sales. Advertising firms have experienced massive waves of layoffs, at first blamed on recession, and now unavoidably attributable to a fundamental decline in the effectiveness of advertising in today's business world. On the promotion side, companies like Procter & Gamble are moving toward everyday low prices to break the cycle of customers buying only when product is on sale.

Perhaps most convincingly, in April 1993, the stock markets went through a significant reevaluation of name-brand companies. When Philip Morris decided to cut the price of Marlboro cigarettes, the stock market was shocked. Philip Morris stock dropped $14.75 a share, or 23 percent, on April 2. The rest of the consumer products industry reasoned that Philip Morris' problems were isolated; consumer products were not so obviously tied to health problems like cancer. As the stock market decided soon after, however, the issue was not the health impact of cigarettes, but the lower premium that name-brand products were likely to command in the future. The market concluded that generics and low-price brands had made a lasting impact on consumer product companies. The result was a broad devaluation of stock prices for a broad range of consumer product companies. In other words, Wall Street devalued the power of brand names to bring customers to the company, ushering in a new era for consumer product companies with different requirements for success.

Another crack in marketing's foundation involves the notion of a market. Much of the brilliance of the marketing concept is due to segmenting customers into groups based on common needs or attributes. From a customer's perspective, however, segmentation is like cattle herding. Customer needs and characteristics are churned through multivariate statistical models, and then customers are herded into clusters and branded with labels such as "do-it-yourselfers," "early adopters," or "accumulators." *At its core, marketing is reductionistic, oversimplifying the reality of what it takes to meet customer needs.* Customers now have the power to demand that they be treated with respect and dignity, as individual entities, both while they are prospects and after they become customers.

One attempt to augment the mass-market approach embraced by marketing is the concept of *one-to-one marketing* in *The One on One Future* introduced by Peppers and Rogers in 1993. While these authors address many relevant issues in dealing with today's customer, the term one-to-one marketing is ultimately an oxymoron; markets are groups of customers, and you can't have a group of one.

RESISTANCE TO CHANGE

How did sales and marketing get into so much trouble? Why did selling to customers become so adversarial? How did marketing become so out of touch with customer needs?

SHORT-TERM ORIENTATION

Many salespeople live from sale to sale, transaction to transaction. They face quarterly quotas and goals. People who spend most of their workday in a series of transactions often find it difficult to shift to a broader perspective. Their work is with the trees, not the forest. In the same way, a transaction orientation dominated manufacturing for years. But manufacturing departments have been breaking out of this rut. For too many companies, the sales force is still in a short-term, transaction-based rut.

Marketing management, while not transaction-oriented, is quarterly report–oriented. The quarterly financial benefits that were such enticing outcomes of splendid marketing initiatives are now distorting good judgment. As the quarter progresses, marketers watch as results fall below plan. In response, they dig into their bag of marketing tricks and find that they need discounts, allowances, and promotions to make ends meet. But the customer is wise to the pattern, and has been waiting for the end of the quarter with the intent to stock up on discounted merchandise. While at one time marketing was able to dramatically enhance the effectiveness of discounting and related practices, marketers now find that the market is wise to their tactics and does not respond as it once did.

INBREEDING

Salespeople usually come into sales at an entry level, and many stay with sales throughout their careers. Only a small number have experience in other functions or any basis for a nonsales or cross-functional perspective. One of the natural sources for cross-fertilization—the marketing function—is usually untapped. Marketers have tended to avoid the trenchwork of sales. This career development barrier between sales and marketing has hurt both functions.

TRAINING AND CONDITIONING

Salespeople are particularly thick-skinned. They are selected and trained to be that way. In the past, their success has depended on the strength of their egos out in the marketplace. They are coached and conditioned to fight, be aggressive, and push back, so they are better equipped to resist change or challenges from the outside. They learn to deal with adversity and rejection, and to work through it to get to the sale. They must face rejection one day and get out and make a big sale the next. It is hard to imagine a job that is more filled with rejection than a sales job.

The resilient, fighting spirit required in sales has a downside. Because salespeople deal with so much risk and change in the outside world and spend so much of their time fighting, they keep right on fighting internally. They resist suggestions to try something new. They counter assertions that change is needed. Plus, salespeople reason that they can always go sell for some other firm. If they don't like the changes coming down the line, they just hop to another firm. Finally, the proponents of change are frequently lower-paid employees from manufacturing or quality departments. Salespeople reason that their way must be right because they are paid more money than those calling for change.

This constant resistance to change creates serious credibility problems for sales. People from other areas of the company now expect sales to have a political, defensive angle. They frequently assume that sales is more concerned with polishing its image than doing the right thing for the organization as a whole.

Lack of Viable Alternatives

Perhaps most importantly, the sales and marketing functions resist change simply because management has failed to provide a realistic and viable alternative vision of managing customer relationships. While alternatives are appearing, new approaches that are aligned with customer needs are much harder to find. This is the challenge for second-generation reengineering: *to provide sales and marketing with a new vision for meeting customer needs that is aligned with where customers are going in the twenty-first century.* Marketing and sales can't craft this new vision alone— they need the help of their customers and the rest of their company to do it.

ENTER THE ENGAGEMENT ERA

The course of business development in this country can be characterized by three eras. The three eras represent three different business philosophies of how to regard the customer. The first era, that of sales-driven companies, gave way to the marketing era. We think the marketing era is now being eclipsed by what we refer to as the *era of engagement*.

In the sales era, the primary focus for getting the product to the customer was performance claims; the actual product offering remained constant. In the marketing era, companies designed products that corresponded with market segment needs. Product profitability became a focus, along with effective use of advertising, promotion, and distribution channels. While different in many respects, both of these approaches emphasized bringing customers to the company.

Today, the key is not bringing more customers to the company, but to bring the company to the customer. By definition, marketing focuses on groups of customers; it is unsuited for building the one-to-one relationships that are now required. At the same time, sales must be completely reengineered and merged with other functions in a new way that brings the company to the customer.

THE ENGAGEMENT PROCESS

According to *Webster's Dictionary*:

engage 1: to offer (as one's word) as security for a debt or cause   2 a: to engage or entrap in or as if in a snare or bog   b: to attract and hold by influence or power   c: to interlock with   3: to bind (as oneself) to do something   4 a: to provide occupation for   b: to arrange to obtain the use or services of: HIRE   5 a: to hold the attention of   b: to induce to partici-pate...

The Webster's definition of *engage* captures much of what com-panies experience today in the business development process. The definition is two-sided; it recognizes both sides of the buy-ing/selling transaction. It acknowledges the buy/sell realities through use of words like "power" and "induce." Most impor-tantly, the term *engage* acknowledges the complexity and "messi-ness" of working with today's customers.

As the engagement era replaces the sales and marketing eras, the company's potential to add value increases. But the engage-ment era is also a more complex form of business development. The migration of business development eras is summarized in Figure 5-1.

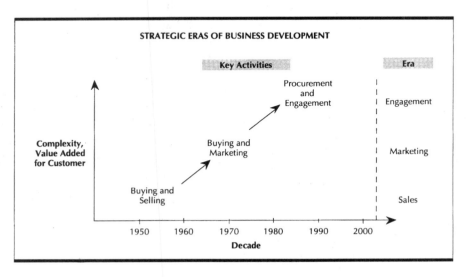

Figure 5-1

In the previous chapter, we discussed how buying has been transformed into a more comprehensive set of processes described as procurement. To effectively work with customers, companies must align their acquisition processes—how they acquire and serve their customers—based on how customers are approaching their procurement objectives. We have aligned the supplier's acquisition processes with the three procurement processes from Chapter 3 to form what we call the engagement process (see Figure 5-2). Note that the procurement and acquisition processes seek the same three primary outcomes: target solutions, contracts, and profit. However, suppliers and customers conduct different activities relative to their unique goals in the engagement process. Also, each process impacts the others. For example, a profitable exchange enhances the likelihood that future solutions will be identified and future contracts will be acquired.

The degree of sophistication and capability that customers and suppliers bring to each process phase and activity differs by

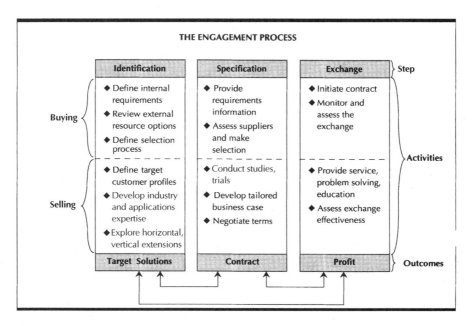

Figure 5-2

industry and situation. Success in today's engagement era requires companies and customers to define processes and agree on common outcomes for each process, and to complete the activities required to accomplish the outcomes. In other words, Figure 5-2 is merely an illustration; it is up to each company and supplier to define how they will proceed through the engagement process, and to align respective activities to ensure that the target outcomes are completed.

As currently configured, most marketing and sales organizations are not geared to conduct this one-on-one process mapping and alignment. While salespeople, at their best, tailor how they work with each customer, the remaining departments in most companies, including marketing, do not. This is where the marketing era ends and the engagement era begins. *To enter the new era, companies need to reengineer their business acquisition processes so that they align with each customer's procurement processes and flex with each customer's requirements.*

THE ENGAGEMENT EQUATION

As the new engagement era focuses on bringing the company to the customer, companies must compete on the basis of numer-

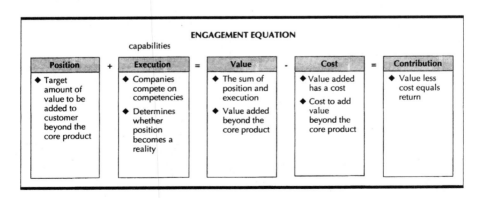

ENGAGEMENT EQUATION

capabilities

Position	+	Execution	=	Value	-	Cost	=	Contribution
◆ Target amount of value to be added to customer beyond the core product		◆ Companies compete on competencies ◆ Determines whether position becomes a reality		◆ The sum of position and execution ◆ Value added beyond the core product		◆ Value added has a cost ◆ Cost to add value beyond the core product		◆ Value less cost equals return

Figure 5-3

ous factors beyond that of core product offering, and they incur much higher costs. How, then, will they be sure to arrive at a satisfactory level of profitability? The engagement equation in Figure 5-3 and the sections that follow illustrate how successful firms ensure that they reach and maintain levels of profitability.

POSITION

Position is the philosophy embraced by a company when describing how it works with its customers. More specifically, position is *the target amount of value to be added to customers beyond the core product during the engagement process.* Parallel to Peter Drucker's recent concept of the "theory of the business" (*Harvard Business Review,* September/October 1994), we think there is a "theory of the engagement." There are numerous ways a company can design its engagement process, and companies can position their engagements to deliver more, equal, or less value than the competition. Two examples illustrate these options.

R. R. DONNELLEY.   R. R. Donnelley, one of the country's largest printing companies, uses a high-value positioning strategy. Where other printers traditionally hand off the responsibility for delivering on the printing contract to service and manufacturing functions, Donnelley's salespeople traditionally provide customers with one point of contact to address any issue that the customer might encounter over the course of their relationship with R. R. Donnelley. In this way, Donnelley positions itself to deliver a higher level of service relative to competitor norms.

IBM SERIES/1.   On the other hand, companies can also position to deliver a lower level of value relative to competitive norms. An example made famous by Theodore Levitt (*The Marketing Imagination,* 1983) is provided by the introduction of the IBM Series/1 minicomputer in the late 1970s. Digital Equipment Corp. (DEC), the dominant player in minicomputers, was using the traditional mainframe approach to selling minicomputers. They designed system configurations and developed application software to help customers obtain attractive returns from costly investments. IBM took a new approach to selling minicomputers. Their position was to let customers use their own resources, or computer consultants, for system design and software development. IBM reasoned that the minicomputer market had been well educated by DEC's sales force, and that numerous resources were available to help customers put well-designed minicomputers to work. IBM designed a technologically reliable machine, and priced it competitively. In a few years' time, IBM made dramatic inroads into the minicomputer market, marking the ultimate decline of DEC as the dominant player in the minicomputer industry.

EXECUTION

Execution captures how well the company implements its position. Companies ultimately compete on execution. Great position and lousy execution yields low value for the customer. This realization has led Lou Gerstner of IBM to assert that "strategy is execution." Companies need to deliver to the customer's expectations for any given engagement position they take, or they suffer a competitive disadvantage. In the R. R. Donnelley and IBM Series/1 cases, these companies chose to differ from the normative approach to engagement. By taking these risks, it was critical for these companies to ensure that they fully executed to customer expectations for their respective positions. The execution concept also captures a subtle reality: companies can achieve significant differentiation in the eyes of the customer simply by outexecuting the competition. To illustrate this point, we will add Procter & Gamble and IBM Mainframe to R. R. Donnelley and IBM Series/1 in our discussion.

R. R. DONNELLEY. Historically, R. R. Donnelley has executed their superior positioning by fielding superior salespeople and giving them the power they need to perform at a higher level than the competition. One tactic used by Donnelley is education; they train their salespeople for two years, which is far beyond typical industry practice. (Competitors know this, and they actively recruit Donnelley salespeople after they complete their training.) Donnelley salespeople also have unique power within the company. They review product as it comes off the printing press and can reject the product if it is not right; they call paper suppliers to obtain price points that are required to complete a deal; they work with plants to obtain production schedules that were previously "unavailable"; they even create new printing divisions when their business ideas warrant it. To make their high-value position work, Donnelley has an ethic that says: "Any customer failure is a sales failure," and (internally) "When a salesperson calls, take the call." These and other principles empower salespeople to deliver on the high value R. R. Donnelley promises.

IBM Series/1. It was probably tempting for IBM to use its highly successful mainframe sales force and engagement approach to sell minicomputers. Instead, IBM set up a separate sales force, staffed it with nonmainframe salespeople, and focused on rapid market penetration. IBM relied on its product technology, price, and brand name to do much of the work. Salespeople concentrated on activity: lots of sales calls. They submitted standardized proposals, with simple purchase and lease options. And salespeople made modest claims about configuration and software support. This high level of emphasis on activity and simplicity, combined with a new sales force not burdened with the traditional assumptions of how to sell computers, were key to executing IBM's low-value position. Customers were obviously willing to accept the low-value approach; they were receiving a quality IBM product that was finally targeted for midsized applications, and salespeople were efficient at securing the product for them—simple expectations were set relative to the engagement, and IBM fully delivered on them.

P&G and IBM Mainframe. One of the most surreptitious ways of competing is by outexecuting the industry's standard engagement process—an approach used by both P&G's and IBM's mainframe sales forces. P&G has been noted for its consistent ability to recruit, hire, and train the best grocery sales force in the country. Their salespeople use P&G on their resume as a ticket to many other opportunities, because of the formidable reputation those salespeople enjoy simply by being a part of the P&G sales force. And these salespeople have proven themselves the best at executing the same sales approaches used by competitors—these salespeople just do it better. The same is true for the sales and service of IBM's mainframes. IBM did not target a different position relative to competitors, they just execute better. Like P&G, IBM excels at recruiting, selecting, and training. They use intelligence tests as a selection tool. They have exceptional training for new hires. They have intensive monitoring of product performance and customer satisfaction. In combination, IBM's mainframe sales and service execution created formidable competitive barriers.

VALUE

Value is *the sum of position and execution.* Since position and execution are focused on the engagement process, the value concept does not include any value to the customer associated with the core product. The interaction between position and execution for R. R. Donnelley, IBM Series/1, P&G, and IBM Mainframe is summarized in Figure 5-4. The lines for R. R. Donnelley illustrate that they have a high position relative to the competition and that customer expectations for the high position are being met, yielding an above-average value delivered to the customer. If R. R. Donnelley regularly delighted customers with its execution of the high position, or if it outdelivered the high position relative to other competitors, its execution would be high, and its value delivered would also be high.

P&G and IBM Mainframe both adopted average positions and excelled at execution, resulting in above-average value delivered. To increase the value of their engagements, these compa-

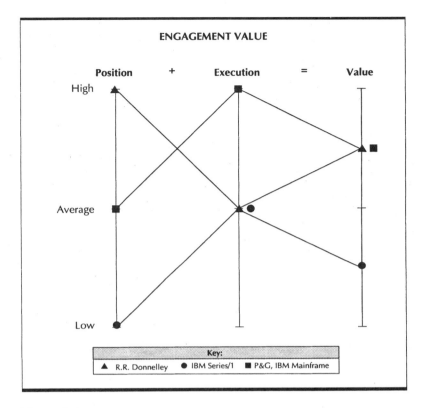

Figure 5-4

nies would need to adopt positions to exceed industry norms.

IBM Series/1 adopted a low position and executed that low position to customer expectations, resulting in below-average value to the customer. For IBM to offset this lower value, it needed to have lower cost per transaction. This indeed was the case, and will be explored next.

Cost

Cost is *the expense directly incurred throughout the engagement.* It is tough to establish a value edge relative to the competition, and it is even tougher to do so· at an affordable cost. In fact, companies can spend so much in the engagement process that their overall company profitability is seriously impacted. As mentioned in Chapter 4, E. F. Hutton is a good example of too much being spent on sales (through sales compensation) relative to results, so that the company was bankrupted.

As engagement value increases in proportion to the value of the core product, it becomes more important to track engagement costs on a per-transaction or per-customer basis. While the marketing era moved us to develop improved product profitability accounting methods, the engagement era requires an accounting of profit by customer, and this profit calculation must include engagement costs. Unfortunately, most companies are not yet ready to track engagement costs down to the transaction or customer; instead, these costs are tracked in aggregate by department and function below the contribution margin line of the income statement.

A number of companies and industries, however, have tracked engagement costs at the transaction and customer level for decades. For example, law and consulting firms typically record engagement costs per customer—they do so by tracking individual time per customer by the hour. The same is true for AT&T teams involved in selling and installing large communications switches; cross-functional teams are formed to secure and initiate new business, and team member project time is tracked and allocated against revenue received from the customer. Many service companies also track engagement costs, since they are a major component of their service cost. The trend toward "knowledge-worker" organizations, combined with the increasing role of engagement value, will make it ever more important for companies to use time accounting or other techniques to track engagement costs and allocate them against transaction or customer.

For IBM Series/1, its lower value relative to DEC needed to be offset with a lower cost relative to DEC; otherwise, IBM would have an uncompetitive cost structure. IBM delivered on this requirement. Its heavy sales activity emphasis yielded higher sales per person than DEC, thus producing a lower cost per transaction than DEC.

CONTRIBUTION

Contribution is *the difference between value and cost.* By examining Figure 5-5, we can see that each company produced above-average contributions, yet different paths were taken to reach this enviable position. For R. R. Donnelley, P&G, and IBM Mainframe, their above-average values, combined with average cost per transaction, yielded above-average contributions. IBM Series/1 ended up with an above-average contribution by com-

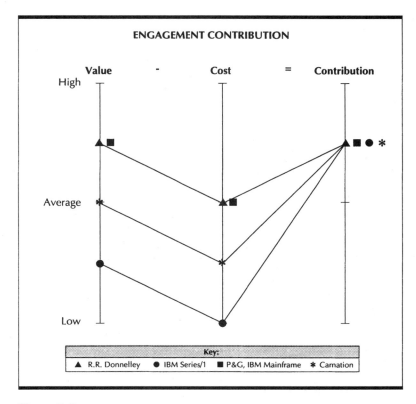

Figure 5-5

bining their below-average value with a very low cost per transaction.

An additional company—the old Carnation company prior to the Nestlé acquisition—was included in Figure 5-5 to illustrate yet another path to above-average contribution. Carnation adopted average position and execution to yield average value. Their uniqueness was in their low cost per transaction, which was achieved by below-market pay per person. Despite the fact that Carnation's low pay made it a target for recruitment by other food companies willing to pay employees more, Carnation was able to maintain acceptable field retention rates by creating a strong team culture. Its recruiting practices focused on creating a homogeneous group, compensation emphasized team results, and ample forms of team recognition were used. In combination with average value, Carnation's low cost per transaction yielded above-average contribution.

THE ENGAGEMENT STRATEGY

Once companies know the contribution made during their engagement process, they can develop a strategy to improve it. The converse of this statement is equally true: if a company does not know its engagement contribution, it is hard to improve it. A major downfall of first-generation reengineering efforts was that they did not adequately define engagement contribution. The traditional reengineering gap analysis of "here is what customers want, here is what we give them, and here is a cost-benefit analysis to justify significant expenditures or layoffs" is inadequate. It is our observation that too many people leading reengineering efforts do not understand how the customer relationships work, they are still wrapped up in the sales or marketing era, they don't understand the components of engagement value, or they do not know how to define engagement contribution.

The five companies we have been tracking in this chapter

will be used now as examples for examining strategic engagement alternatives.

R. R. DONNELLEY.   R. R. Donnelley could achieve still higher contribution by reducing its costs. While the two-year training period eventually yields highly effective salespeople, trainees have low productivity during their first two years. This decreases overall sales per person and increases Donnelley's costs. By assigning trainees to senior salespeople, Donnelley potentially could increase the productivity of senior salespeople and accelerate trainee development at the same time.

Alternatively, Donnelley could reengineer to enhance the execution of its high position. Such an effort might involve the formation of dedicated teams performing sales, service, prepress, manufacturing, and delivery functions for assigned groups of customers.

IBM SERIES/1 AND CARNATION.   IBM and Carnation do not have many options for improving their contributions. Their transaction costs were already very low, and it is not likely that they could produce more value given the limitations created by their cost positions. They can be satisfied with above-average contributions, or completely reconfigure into very high value operations—a high-risk, low-probability-of-success option.

P&G.   One alternative for companies competing on execution strength is to target higher positions and execute them with distinction equal to that of their current position. For P&G, this could entail a merger of marketing and sales positions to create highly tailored promotional arrangements with customers. Instead, we know that P&G chose a different option: to reduce its engagement value by adopting everyday low prices and significantly reducing trade expenditures. This would likely drop its value to average, at best, and costs per transaction would need to drop significantly to offset the decline in value. Given the commodity nature of the grocery industry and the declining value of brands, the recent P&G strategy is probably well advised.

IBM MAINFRAME. IBM also enjoyed above-average contribution from an above-average value, average cost engagement strategy. IBM could also target a higher position and execute it with distinction, or it could take the P&G route and reduce value and cost. The complication for IBM was a rapidly eroding market. So, its lifelong-employment and no-layoffs philosophy made it difficult to keep engagement costs in line with a shrinking market. As we know, IBM eventually had to make massive layoffs to reestablish a competitive cost structure. Now, with Integrated Systems Solutions Corporation (ISSC) in the lead, IBM is adopting a very high position and seeking to execute it with traditional excellence. Unfortunately, the mainframe market is now so fragmented that it is difficult for IBM to take a generalist approach. Instead, IBM has been forced to target specific industries, thus reducing the shadow it once cast, but increasing its ability to execute a high engagement position.

WHAT THE NEW ERA BRINGS

As companies grow impatient with the functional thinking of the two previous sales and marketing eras and attempt to better cope with today's customers, alternatives to traditional sales and marketing functions are being explored. Companies are finding viable new approaches. Several scenarios of how companies are moving out of their traditional sales and marketing orientations into customer-driven approaches are described in the following sections.

TAILORED PRODUCT OFFERINGS

Value added beyond the core product has grown dramatically in many industries over the past decade. In a world where technological advances remain current for only six to nine months, competing on the basis of the core product is not enough. To maintain profitability, companies are now forced to add significant value beyond the core product or to dramatically cut engagement costs, thereby allowing them to cut their core product prices.

As argued in previous chapters, customers assume that suppliers can provide products with competitive features and prices. Often, the competitive arena surrounds what companies wrap around the core product. This is where the one-to-one tailoring takes place in the new engagement era, as illustrated in Figure 5-6.

The key to enduring competitive success with customers is to manage the total product offering. Companies can add value to the core product and obtain an appropriate premium for this total offering. Or they can limit core product additions and transfer the associated cost savings to the customer in the form of a lower price. The important point of departure from the marketing to the engagement era is *additions to the core product must be tailored to the individual customer.*

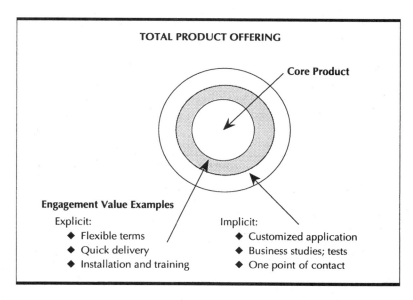

Figure 5-6

How can companies provide different total product offerings to every customer? First, tailoring requires field personnel who constantly identify which customers value only the core product and which customers value engagement services. No tailoring is required for core-product-only customers, and perhaps the company will choose not to work with these customers. Second, acquisition team members are given responsibility for customer profitability and with this responsibility comes the authority to tailor engagement services to fit the customer. This is executing the classic "bring decision making closer to the customer" philosophy. Third, companies may choose to tailor with their largest customers first, then move the approach down through middle-tier customers.

PARTNERSHIPS AND SINGLE-SOURCING

As the boundaries between buyers and sellers become more transparent and permeable, the sales function—once charged with pushing through that boundary—becomes less relevant. As more and more buyers seek close and enduring relationships with suppliers through partnerships or single-source arrangements and longer contracts, the need for salespeople performing the traditional sales jobs diminishes.

There is no real selling or marketing in partnerships or single-sourcing arrangements with long-term contracts. The focus is on *managing the relationship,* which is an executive and multifunctional job. As the number of partnerships and long-term contracts increases, individuals devoted to selling new accounts become less and less important.

SUBCONTRACTING OUT SALES WORK

Over the past two decades, companies have increasingly turned to subcontracting; they are outsourcing work that becomes too costly or too difficult to perform in-house. Sales and marketing functions can be subcontracted out in the same way and for the same reasons as any number of other functions. If the sales force is not productive, or its costs are too high, or the value created is not sufficient, sales can be outsourced. As sales becomes less prominent within the organization, using a rep firm becomes more feasible. Companies may contract out for all sales work, or keep a greatly reduced sales force for acquisitions only and contract out the rest.

There are professional sales forces that sell their services to other companies. A professional sales company in Los Angeles, for example, recruits students from the Mormon-affiliated Brigham Young University every summer. These students form a highly homogeneous sales force with strong values. They sell pest-control services door to door in Los Angeles for Terminix. Terminix has found that these salespeople are more productive and cost less on a per transaction basis.

Or companies can outsource marketing tasks upstream to their suppliers. Just as Wal-Mart requires its suppliers to perform merchandising and inventory management functions that were previously completed internally, companies can ask their suppliers to conduct new product research or perform other marketing functions that the company would otherwise perform on its own.

Shifting to Other Channels

If a direct sales force becomes too burdensome or relatively unprofitable, management can eliminate or reduce its direct sales force and shift to other sales channels. Numerous companies have reduced direct sales work while expanding telemarketing, direct mail, electronic selling, or some combination of alternative channels.

In an extreme example, Dell has had great success selling computers by direct mail—a channel that was utterly rejected by major players in the computer industry less than a decade ago. Dell has built a huge volume of business not only on the basis of its product but also on the basis of a distribution channel that saves consumers time and money.

Medco (recently acquired by Merck) has built a large business in mail-order prescriptions, replacing retail pharmacy services that were once considered an indispensable part of consumer life. Meanwhile, QVC is quickly demonstrating that electronic shopping may displace retail, telemarketing, and direct-mail channels for a number of consumer goods. Also, a number of insurance companies have expanded their telemarketing groups while shrinking their direct sales forces.

MERGING FUNCTIONS

It is quite possible that the functions being performed by sales or marketing could be subsumed into other functions. One example is provided by Kao Corporation, Japan's $6.1 billion toiletry company. At Kao, marketing has merged with R&D, and this merged group represents one-fourth of Kao's employees. Other companies, like Herman Miller, assign top executives the additional responsibility for managing select accounts or prospects, sometimes without the help of a salesperson. In both of these cases, the marketing or sales function is integrated into another function. While sound marketing or sales principles are still utilized, they are assumed to be part of good management, and do not require a separate function to be implemented.

VIRTUAL MINICOMPANIES

In both the sales and the marketing eras, a function within the company drove the company. In the customer-driven era, companies are exploring totally different business management philosophies. Some companies have been very successful in the past by creating aggressive, performance-oriented cultures, with sales at the heart of their organizations. But companies can never go back to selling as the sole interface with the customer, because the new era requires contact between the customer and more than one function within the supplier's organization; no single function can provide a stand-alone interface with the customer.

To address the problem, companies are focusing on building partnerships among corporate functions. This perspective acknowledges that a company builds its capability to partner with customers by facilitating teamwork across its own functional areas. Hence, companies like 3M allow their researchers to take successful innovations to market and head up the resulting new business ventures. Or, companies like American Express create groups like the "Office of the Chairman" to limit parochialism. Others, such as Levi Strauss, establish aspirations statements that emphasize trust, relationships, respect, and teamwork (for example, see *Harvard Business Review,* September–October 1990). Still others, such as the Mayo Clinic, adopt participative decision making through committees (see a special report on the Mayo Clinic in *Perspectives,* Sibson & Company, Vol. III, No. 1).

Yet the cross-functional concept may not be enough. It still relies on specialization, rather than fully satisfying the customer. Companies have tried for years to create seamless service to customers across functions, and they are still searching.

A virtual minicompany is a dedicated team of individuals with different areas of expertise who also are broadly versed in other team members' specialties. Team members are jointly responsible for meeting the needs of a group of customers and for producing target levels of profitability for the company.

Examples of virtual minicompanies are found in printing (R. R. Donnelley) and computer chips (Intel), where manufacturing cells are built around a set of customers. The cells are then augmented with other support positions to work with customers to ensure that their needs are met over the life of the customer relationship.

CONCLUSIONS

Entering the engagement era is not an option; we are in it. Customers have reengineered their procurement process, and suppliers need to align their acquisition process in response. The significant opportunity available in today's engagement era is targeting and executing an engagement strategy that creates superior contribution for the company. This is done by one of two alternatives:

1. Adding value to the core product in a way that differentiates the company from the competition at an affordable cost (for example, R. R. Donnelley, P&G).

2. Taking costs out of the engagement process, so that lower prices can be charged to customers, or engagement efficiency and productivity will be greatly enhanced (for example, IBM Series/1, Carnation).

DISCONNECTS AND POTENTIAL

As Bob Vila would tell us, we now have the beginnings of a dream house. We know a lot about how the ground beneath us is shifting through our discussion of the failure of functions and the power shift. We know something about the concept for a great new house through our discussion of the new engagement era and what it brings. We already have a lot of raw material lying about in the form of existing marketing and sales functions. And we have a powerful new tool—reengineering—to help us build a better house.

What we don't have is a description of exactly what might be wrong with our existing house, how to find what is wrong, and what might be required to fix the problem. This is especially important when a tool as powerful as reengineering can do as much damage as any jackhammer or chainsaw when applied to the wrong part of the house.

We believe that there is a logical sequence to finding opportunities for improving your firm's approach to managing its customers. Too many reengineering efforts on customer-facing processes have failed because their sponsors have not asked the question, "Reengineer for what competitive advantage?" They have identified hosts of process improvement ideas and have failed to consider them within a strategic context.

Avoiding the trap of reengineering without building an enduring advantage requires using tools. The remainder of this book provides these tools, starting with the disconnects and the engagement potential tools.

DISCONNECTS

The disconnects tool challenges three core assumptions that were effective in the previous marketing and selling eras: the viability of functional excellence, mass marketing, and cross-functional coordination. Testing for these disconnects can help determine whether a company is trapped in a bygone era.

THE FUNCTIONAL EXCELLENCE DISCONNECT

The first disconnect is adhering to the belief that a superior sales force or marketing department can lead a company to competitive advantage in the year 2000. A single function, no matter how good, just can't do the work required to meet customer needs in the new engagement era. The full company must serve the customer in a coordinated fashion; a single function can no longer stand as a core competency for a company.

In 1954, Peter Drucker asserted, "There is only one valid definition of business purpose: To create a customer" (*Practice of Management*). For many companies, sales and marketing functions have played this philosophy to its end, and now the engagement era demands that companies go beyond creating customers and focus more broadly on serving and retaining customers.

SALES

Just because the top line on the income statement deals with sales does not mean that we need a function charged with responsibility for that line. One function alone cannot be responsible for the top line of the income statement. Customers don't tolerate it, and it isn't working.

"Sales" is too narrow a concept for a function charged with the responsibility for managing interactions with customers. Sales' natural bent to acquire customers often leaves little room for a long-term perspective or a partnership orientation with customers—an orientation in which there is lots of give-and-take, a win-win attitude, and a willingness to marshal the company's resources to meet customer needs.

Often those responsible for creating customers ignore important line items further down the income statement, such as costs. Interactions with customers cost money; so do exchanges of goods and services. Can someone charged with the responsibility for building customer interactions be regarded as blameless for the associated costs? Of course not, but the sales concept is focused on the top, not the bottom line, forcing too many sales forces to ignore the cost component of customer interactions.

MARKETING

Many marketers helped their companies to better manage product profitability by conducting rigorous predictions of how customer segments would respond to a product and how much would be sold at a given price. Marketing expertise is no longer enough. It is an important augmentation to the sales concept, but it also is functionally rooted and "siloistic." That is, marketing is too vertically focused on its own area of expertise. It does not address the multifaceted, coordinated effort required to meet customer needs through an evolving, dynamic relationship. It does not coordinate all of the cross-functional processes and expertise required to deliver to customers as promised. It is still rooted in creating customers, rather than in doing the one-on-one work required to keep them.

THE MASS MARKETS DISCONNECT

The second disconnect is contained in the myth that a product can be mass marketed to preeminence. While there will be exceptions, mass marketing will not be the norm it was in the sixties and seventies. Mass marketing is a concept that has served its time. The mentality of mass marketing works against what needs to happen with today's customers—that is, customization.

Companies must embrace the customization concept as part of doing business. Customization does not necessarily imply that a different product is manufactured for every customer. It does mean, however, that all customers are different, so their different problems need to be solved through the engagement. Participants in the engagement process must embrace the responsibility for solving the customers' unique problems or creating unique opportunities for them.

Once the customization philosophy is embraced, it becomes obvious for many companies that the old ways of managing marketing and sales do not work. Sales and marketing need to merge so that customer-by-customer customization can be done in a profitable manner. Decisions that once were strictly protected as marketing-only domain—product features, price, promotional spending—now must be brought closer to the customer.

PRODUCT DESIGN

For product design, customization in the customer-driven era means broader involvement, which includes the customer. Product design was a marketing-exclusive effort in the past, and that error is costly today. Valuable feedback and ideas from other functions and the customer are missed and companies incorrectly conclude that they can split the differences among customers by using a compromised product design. Those who are directly involved with the customer are aware of competitive successes and failures, what works and what doesn't. These people will tell you that compromises have consequences. The people with the relevant customer and competitor information must be involved in product design. This includes all customer-facing positions, as well as the customer. This broad-based approach represents the new approach to product design.

At the same time, during product design, a broad business perspective (encompassing concerns such as profitability and return on investment) needs to be maintained. Marketing has fulfilled this responsibility in the past. Now, the challenge is for marketing to convey the broad business perspective to those in direct contact with the customer. This is so that those in contact can be more effective, not only as participants in the product design process, but also in managing the entire customer engagement process.

PRICING AND PROMOTION

Pricing and promotion decisions also must be brought closer to the customer by involving customer-facing positions. The traditional, centralized, and bureaucratic approach to making these decisions is no longer effective. Customers demand timely decisions that are tailored to their business needs. Companies have tried to make pricing and promotion decision work by funneling everything in through marketing. This is not working because marketing is not close enough to the engagement to anticipate how pricing and promotion decisions made from headquarters will impact the engagement. When companies realize that they must price the total product offering and respond to each competitive situation, they realize that these decisions must be decentralized and brought closer to the customer.

There are important profitability considerations, as well as regulatory issues, to manage when pricing and promotion decisions are being made. But these factors need not be addressed through marketing. Instead, marketing and the other customer-facing positions can partner to ensure that profits and regulations are well managed while customer customization is the focus of attention.

This approach to decision-making processes that were previously managed exclusively by the marketing department carries with it a completely new role for marketers. Now, they need to act as coaches and facilitators. They are also responsible for generating customer-specific information on profitability that can be used by the customer-facing positions to make appropriate product, price, and promotion decisions.

Some marketing departments have addressed customization by jointly assuming responsibility for customer acquisition with their sales organizations. When this approach is taken, the traditional barriers between the two functions diminish, and one group is seen as actively helping the other. Some marketing departments within AT&T have taken this approach, and not only is there a higher success rate in penetrating target industries and introducing new product applications and solutions, but also, marketing is viewed as a critical partner by the field sales organizations.

THE CROSS-FUNCTIONAL DISCONNECT

The third disconnect is subscribing to the myth that engagements can succeed with a cross-functional approach to organizing a company's employees. In reality, responsibilities for managing the process cannot be cleanly divided into distinct functions because customers do not work that way. Customer approaches to buying are "messy"—not easy to label or categorize. The procurement process has no neat start or end. Customers start anywhere in the three sets of processes, jump back and forth in a nonlinear manner, and simultaneously move forward in some processes while moving backwards in others.

This level of complexity simply is too much to coordinate across functions. Companies pretend to organize around their customers by creating cross-functional teams, but they still manage functionally. While cross-functional teams represent a step forward, they alone are not the answer. A major health-care manufacturer—Baxter—has adopted numerous team approaches over the years to coordinate its interactions with its customers across numerous product and service divisions. This company will be the first to tell you that they are not satisfied with the result.

The problem is that the theory of cross-functional teams is a stopgap measure. It stops short of creating a dedicated team to serve the customer or groups of customers. Cross-functional teams go halfway toward bringing the company to the customer. Companies that go all the way with dedicated teams will have the advantage.

ENGAGEMENT POTENTIAL

After breaking with some old assumptions of what works with customers, companies need to explore the potential of what value can be added to customers during each phase of the engagement process. In the following sections, we examine the tremendous potential within the identification, specification, and exchange processes. A number of ideas are provided to stimulate thinking as companies define their engagement potential. We want to stress, however, that different companies have significantly different engagement opportunities. Each company must creatively explore its own engagement potential. The following ideas can be used as idea starters.

IDENTIFICATION

The primary objective of the identification process is to find opportunities that match the company's target solutions. Some critical activities in the identification process are developing industry and applications expertise, establishing efficient replenishment, exploring horizontal and vertical extensions, and defining target-customer profiles. We will also discuss some important tools that support the identification process.

INDUSTRY EXPERTISE

An important value that can be delivered during the identification process is industry expertise. Companies develop industry expertise by conducting in-depth studies of specific types of problems and by doing a lot of work for that industry. Industry studies may yield valuable technical specifications that are not otherwise available from other suppliers. Consequently, the supplier adds value to the customer by becoming expert on certain aspects of the customer's operational or marketing requirements.

The other major value of developing industry expertise comes from the supplier being so well versed in the industry that its customer-coverage personnel have a learning curve about the customer's business that is as short as possible. A supplier's customer-coverage personnel can demonstrate industry knowledge all during the customer's procurement process through their response time and decision-making effectiveness, providing a significant competitive advantage. Consequently, as the supplier develops unique solutions for the customer, the supplier is leveraging off of previous industry experience, rather than using experience with the customer to learn about the industry.

Enhancing industry expertise involves developing proprietary information, generating materials that demonstrate industry expertise, and bringing industry expertise to the customer.

PROPRIETARY INFORMATION.   Industry data that can be converted into the kinds of insight that lead to inquiries and leads needs to be gathered. To do so, the identification team must gather information from existing customers in the industry, or survey broader sets of prospects and customers in a target industry. Insightful questions about how the firm's products can be used to enhance the wealth-creation processes of its prospects and customers need to be asked, and the resulting information needs to be cataloged so that it can be analyzed. The skills required to develop, maintain, and utilize proprietary databases may need to be acquired from the outside or developed from within.

MATERIALS.   Articles, press releases, speeches, and seminars need to be written. Brochures and audiovisuals need to be produced. Reengineering may need to design the required decision-making, prioritizing, and approval processes for completing these materials. What does the material need to look like to best support the customer-coverage teams? What publications and public forums should be targeted?

BRINGING INDUSTRY EXPERTISE TO THE CUSTOMER.   Perhaps the most important question related to generating industry information and materials is "Who will do the work?" Members of the identification team should be involved; this builds and establishes their industry expertise. There is nothing more credible than true industry experts working directly with customers.

Unfortunately, true industry expertise is acquired over time, person by person. It is not acquired at training seminars, but through on-the-job experience with customers in the industry. Training can accelerate the learning process, but it cannot replace customer experience.

Consequently, career development plans are required so the desired expertise is built and then converted into manifestations of the expertise. Companies can signal a true commitment to target industries by preparing these development plans and then providing individuals with support (for example, access to communications experts) to convert their industry experiences into true manifestations of industry expertise.

APPLICATIONS EXPERTISE

Another activity that generates value during the identification process is providing customers with applications expertise. Customers need proven analytical and diagnostic tools to assess operations and develop improvements. By applying such tools, a solution can be designed that is tailored to the customer's operation and includes all of the necessary support, such as training, maintenance, and technical manuals. Applications expertise can be delivered to customers through integrated solutions, proprietary analytical tools, and experienced applications specialists.

INTEGRATED SOLUTIONS.   Making the shift from selling products to providing customers with integrated applications that solve problems is difficult. Specific business operations need to be targeted, and expertise in improving performance through various types of applications needs to be established. The emphasis in these efforts is to design a tailored solution that draws on whatever resources are necessary to solve the customer's problem, including the customer's resources as well as those of other vendors. Some consulting firms, such as Andersen Consulting, have made significant systems investments. These investments allow their consultants to access client studies so that earlier solutions can be examined, perfected, and applied to new client problems.

PROPRIETARY ANALYTICAL TOOLS.   One clear form of applications expertise is an analytical tool that is unique to a specific type of operation. Some analytical tools take the form of a series of diagnostics that are designed to ensure that the optimal application is customized for the customer. Cincinnati Milacron and Bell and Howell are firms that pair engineering analysts with their sales personnel. This pairing starts the sales process with a free diagnostic of a manufacturing customer's throughput per production line. Other tools are conceptual frameworks that guide the assessment of the customer's business operation. Still others provide customers with mechanisms for tracking a specific business operation in a manner that documents the effectiveness of the installed application. Pitney Bowes conducts an extensive analysis of a firm's mail and postage usage patterns before recommending solutions, savings, or financing packages.

BRINGING APPLICATIONS EXPERTISE TO THE CUSTOMER.   Again, the individuals working with the customer are critical to the delivery of applications expertise. They can use sophisticated analytical tools ineffectively, or they can use them to initiate an engagement with the customer that results in the identification of high value-added solutions. As was true with industry expertise, career development plans play a major role in developing applications expertise. While training programs can increase awareness of vendors to potentially use in designing solutions, experienced practitioners must train novices, application by application and customer by customer, until they acquire the depth of expertise required to design integrated solutions.

EFFICIENT REPLENISHMENT

As a rule, the most important business opportunities are with current customers. Identification costs can be four to five times higher for new customers than they are for securing further work with existing customers. The primary choices for pursuing additional business with existing customers are *replenishments* and *extensions*. Replenishment activities are especially relevant for products with shorter life cycles. Reengineering to improve the replenishment activities typically focuses on developing automated order-entry systems, and utilizing lower-cost distribution approaches.

After customers have successful experiences with a firm's product, they may be interested in more efficient ways to handle repeat purchases. Sometimes this involves transferring to customers the responsibility and capability to place orders. For example, remote customer access to order-entry systems and inventory levels are ways to expedite cumbersome, error-prone, and costly order-entry procedures.

Reengineering efforts can also improve the firm's productivity by better utilizing lower-cost distribution channels. The challenge is to cut distribution costs, yet maintain, or even enhance, both customer satisfaction and revenue levels. Ordering and shipping channels such as direct mail and telemarketing are lower-cost alternatives to direct sales, but many problems have been encountered when companies have shifted sales responsibility to these channels. For example, competition and conflict between direct sales and other channels have resulted in less than satisfactory results in many companies.

In these situations, traditional channel structures need to be replaced by teams dedicated to maximizing volume with assigned sets of customers or territories. These arrangements bypass competitive channel-versus-channel behaviors and place a much stronger emphasis on the customer.

HORIZONTAL AND VERTICAL EXTENSIONS

The two primary ways to extend business within an account are horizontally and vertically. Horizontal extensions seek to take the same or similar solutions or applications from one part of the company to another—for example, moving from one plant to another within the same company with the same or similar applications. Horizontal extensions focus on developing a broad base of relationships among company executives so that a broader market for the company's products and services can be established.

Vertical business extensions are ways of adding more value to the customer. They provide broader service solutions that expand to a greater portion of the customer's business. For example, a company first sells an application in payroll, and then targets a comprehensive human resources system application. Vertical extensions focus on leveraging information gathered from narrower applications to build stronger business cases for broader solutions. The company can also seek to leverage relationships built while executing the initial solution to investigate broader applications.

TARGET-CUSTOMER PROFILES: WHO IS A GOOD MATCH?

Sometimes the hardest task in sales and marketing is to define who is *not* a good customer. By reviewing information from other engagement processes, it is possible to develop profiles of customers that will have the longest tenure, have the highest satisfaction with the company, and, accordingly, become most profitable for the company.

Targeting profiles of customers who are likely to be profitable and loyal is particularly important when considering how much to invest in a new customer. It is harder to walk away from "over-the-transom" business that is a poor fit than it is to find and win those customers who are a good match with the company's strengths. For example, if a company has a cost/price leader strategy, then prospects who are partnership-oriented may not be a good fit. Conversely, prospects with a low-cost supplier orientation frequently are not good fits for companies seeking to differentiate on value-added services of their core product.

The following questions illustrate the type of guidelines that help companies with limited resources develop target customer profiles.

- Are large or small customers more profitable?
- Do the most profitable customers start out small and grow, or do they start out large?
- Do our best customers have particular types of operations, or particular types of management philosophies?

If the cost, quality, and speed goals of a reengineering effort are to be reached, it is critical to identify what makes for a good customer, because these characteristics will define the company's strengths and conserve the firm's resources. It also helps ensure that the increasingly greater amount of investment it takes to convert a prospect to a customer is spent on those prospects with the greatest chances of yielding an attractive return for the company.

IDENTIFICATION SUPPORT TOOLS

While some companies develop effective industry or product market plans, many fall short when it comes to developing the tools needed to execute the opportunity identification process effectively at the grass-roots level. Some of the tools that determine success or failure and are particularly important when reengineering the identification process are customer profitability data, qualified leads, market databases, and communications support.

CUSTOMER PROFITABILITY DATA. Salespeople cannot help the company select the right business to acquire if they don't have the right information about market potential, prospects, and current customer profitability. Unfortunately, the typical pattern in companies today is that executives blame salespeople for selling unprofitable business, and at the same time do not give customer profitability reports to their salespeople. On the one hand it is not hard to see what is wrong with this picture. On the other, however, it is very hard to develop customer profitability information that is useful for engagement managers.

Much of today's customer profitability reporting (when it is available, which is not often) is mired in manufacturing variances and corporate allocations. These "green eyeshade" approaches to customer profitability reporting were not designed with making customer decisions in mind. When a company jumps from simple revenue to fully allocated profit reporting by customer, a number of things happen. First, manufacturing variances on a job-by-job or customer basis are often extremely volatile, thus making profit measurement something of a random walk, from the engagement manager's perspective.

Second, many expenses allocated down to a customer level can be full of errors, or highly arbitrary, For example, the task of allocating manufacturing variances to specific jobs or marketing expenses to specific customers is often arbitrary, and processes and systems for tracking these expenses can be highly suspect and susceptible to error.

Reengineering efforts need to develop customer profitability measures that are useful, and avoid the problems that can be associated with expense allocation.

QUALIFIED LEADS. Lead programs must generate prospective leads that are qualified before being distributed to the field for action. Leads are qualified relative to target or industry market, and then calibrated to discern the potential match between the specific prospect and the type of customer the company is looking for. A variety of techniques can be used to qualify leads, and their effectiveness should be validated over time through the use of statistical tests.

MARKET DATABASES. Engagement managers need a thorough understanding of their market if they are to do an effective job of identifying the best opportunities for the company. They need far more than listings of companies in their areas along with descriptive company information including address, lines of business, and officer names and titles.

COMMUNICATIONS. During the opportunity identification process, engagement managers need and rely on materials such as:

1. Detailed results from industry analyses and descriptions of proprietary analytical tools for designing tailored product applications.
2. Case studies of typical industry-specific problems that were solved by the company in previous applications, or common operational problems that have been solved through applications using the company's products.
3. Guidelines describing the operating philosophy and differential advantages of the prospect company, thereby initiating the process of assessing the degree of match between the prospect and the supplier company.
4. Information systems that track the efforts made during the identification process. For example, mailings and telemarketing follow-up calls need to be tracked to:
   a. Collect information such as company name, address, contact name, title, and so forth.
   b. Coordinate efforts among the other groups involved in opportunity identification (for example, direct mail, telemarketing, direct sales).
   c. Track the expenditures and assess the effectiveness of various identification efforts.

SPECIFICATION

The next stage in building the customer asset base is the specification process, previously known as "closing the sale." The supplier makes presentations and proposals, offers trials, makes revisions, and closes the sale with an order. But meanwhile, all throughout this process, the customer not only is purchasing a product or service but is also delineating how the relationship will be assessed over time and how future purchases are to take place. The customer defines their purchasing strategies—these strategies determine whether they want to work with a specified supplier, a preferred supplier, a sole source, a partner, or simply an undifferentiated price/performance supplier. The supplier must determine where it stands with the customer, attempt to modify this position if necessary, and then develop a strategy to pursue future rebuys, lock out the competition, or take the next steps in building the relationship with the customer.

Some critical activities in the specification process include developing substantial customer relationships, conducting customer studies and trials, preparing proposals and rebuy criteria, creating effective specification teams, and providing specification support tools.

SUBSTANTIAL CUSTOMER RELATIONSHIPS

Many customers are tired of the old techniques of building relationships. Customers are less willing to be entertained and to spend time on social interactions with business contacts. Simultaneously, suppliers are finding that business-based social interactions yield limited returns—golfing buddies are not the reliable customers they once were.

Today's customer relationships must be more substantial. A standard we suggest using to gauge the quality of a customer relationship is whether the engagement manager is regarded as a *trusted advisor*. This criterion is not intended to suggest that the engagement manager's expertise, either in designing solutions or relaying industry expertise, is unimportant. However, expertise generates respect, not a relationship. Trusted advisors find that their opinions are sought on matters that do not directly pertain to their particular areas of expertise. The role of trusted advisor includes responding to customer requests for business and career advice, or providing customers with insights into competitive situations and guidance on company decision-making processes. Engagement managers with the capability to be trusted advisors are highly effective at identifying and specifying opportunities.

Engagement managers perform the role of trusted advisor in a number of ways:

1. Interact with a wide variety of individuals within a customer's operation to gather a broad "soft database" on how the company operates, what its values are, and what works within management and at the grass-roots level.

2. Constantly gather information from primary customer contacts on the issues they are facing over the course of performing their jobs.

3. Combine these two sources of information to make astute observations, pose alternative ways of dealing with situations, and help customer contacts assess their alternatives and find the best approach to problems.

In the preceding description, engagement managers use their broad base of contacts within the company to assemble a unique perspective on their customers' business operations. Other individuals who achieve trusted-advisor status begin by understanding how top executives operate across a number of companies and industries. They then integrate these understandings and utilize them as a foundation for providing customers with advice and insights.

Customer Studies

A unique hallmark of modern procurement is the willingness of prospective customers to provide suppliers with the information those suppliers need to assess the prospective customer's unique needs. Potential suppliers differentiate themselves by the penetrating nature of the questions they ask, the data they request, and the analyses they perform. Clearly the insider should have the inside track here. While a supplier, they should have been building a soft database to assess the need for solution redesign. However, if the incumbent has been lax, the aspirant can expose the incumbent's weaknesses and use this as a foundation for dismissal. With an eye to the future, customer studies should follow a format that can be repeated once the company becomes a supplier. This format then serves as an assessment of how well the supplier is performing and whether midcourse corrections are needed.

Ideally, customer studies collect data that are compared to those industry or application benchmarks that were established during the identification process. Customer studies best include a combination of hard and soft customer data. The hard data consists of operation statistics, preferably gathered by the supplier. For example, GE places information chips on various power distribution and control products (for example, motors, electrical switches) to gather information and produce statistics on the customer's manufacturing line. GE also uses its maintenance and service operation to gather additional information about the customer, which can then be analyzed and used in efforts to solve additional customer problems. IBM has used this same technique for decades, attaching chips on their peripherals to gather statistics on service levels.

The soft data includes interviews with key members of the prospect's procurement decision team. Interviews can include a combination of structured and open-ended questions to profile the customer, the customer's needs, and the opportunities to add value as a new supplier. The interviewers would spend some time conveying key messages about the potential supplier's strengths, but should concentrate on information gathering.

If a prospect does not wish to provide information to support a customer study, the company must ask itself if it wants to proceed with pursuing the prospect. Refusal to allow a customer study need not be a reason to automatically close the door on prospect pursuit. But the refusal sends important information about the customer. Perhaps an appropriate level of trust has not been established, or it may be too early in the relationship to expect an exchange of confidential information. Some customers reveal what they view to be highly confidential information only after prospective suppliers have qualified on test projects or later in their procurement process.

PROPOSALS AND REBUY CRITERIA

If a proposal is made to communicate the full value being offered to the customer, then it must specify the company's total product offering. While many companies have developed solid techniques for developing a pro forma income statement on the economic impact of a product application, the more difficult aspects of these proposals are documenting the value of the intangibles surrounding service responsiveness, the potential for the customer's wealth creation process, the supply firms' reputation, and so on. Ideally, communicating the value of the total product offering is done by case studies and comparisons to industry studies and benchmarks.

An outline of the customer's criteria for a rebuy should be integrated into proposals when possible. Inclusion of rebuy criteria sets the expectation that the supplier is committed to, and will be involved in, assessing their own performance. This orientation further communicates the company's commitment to a long-term relationship. In situations where the need for a rebuy is unclear, the criteria for becoming a preferred supplier can be established. If these ideas are not appropriate, then companies need to be sure to establish how customer satisfaction will be assessed. Often, this can be determined by asking the customer which of their supplier relationships work best and for what reasons.

TRIALS

Sometimes the best data for preparing final value proposals comes from product trials. This is especially true since the quality movement has established testing as an integral part of the continuous improvement process, and prospective suppliers fuel their efforts by proposing that new solutions or applications be tested. If trials are a proven way to gain access and build long-term relationships, then they should be a central part of the specification process. On the other hand, if trials tend to be a technique for customers to acquire free consulting, then trials should be used only after the customer passes a number of other qualification hurdles during the customer specification process.

SPECIFICATION TEAMS

More and more, firms are finding that it is no longer possible to acquire business with "lone rangers." Often, personnel from multiple functions are required to conduct the customer studies and trials, and to construct the proposals and rebuy criteria necessary to acquire business. At no time is this truer than when a customer must be pulled away from the preferred supplier.

Specification occurs during the second phase of the engagement process. New business specification teams, or pursuit teams, need to be tailored for each opportunity. Teams must be able to respond quickly to emerging and changing dynamics during the pursuit of new business. Customers may change what they are looking for, or the competition may create the need to modify the plan for winning the business. In many cases, the cost of the efforts necessary to acquire business needs to be reevaluated or requalified in light of emerging information about the customer's operations or buying preferences.

At the same time, pursuit teams can be composed of people

who work together infrequently or are meeting for the first time. Roles need to be established quickly and must be flexible during the life of the specification team.

Cross-functional and cross-discipline specification teams must be coordinated, consequently creating a high demand for team leadership skills. The pursuit team needs a leader, and these leaders need to grasp and communicate the big picture of what the company and the prospect are trying to do strategically. Team leaders frequently need to enlist support from various parts of the company. They assemble their teams based on the given opportunity's requirements. Often, many team members do not report directly within the field sales organization, so the resources are "borrowed" or assigned to help win the business. The team leader's and the company's ultimate success in winning the opportunity can depend on the team leader's reputation, as well as on his or her ability to inspire and build an exciting case for the opportunity and how it can be won.

SUPPORT TOOLS FOR THE SPECIFICATION PROCESS

A number of tools can significantly increase the effectiveness of the specification process, including relationship-building skill development, cost and profit information, customer study and proposal formats, databases, and communications.

RELATIONSHIP-BUILDING SKILL DEVELOPMENT.   While it is one thing to *identify* the need for additional relationship-building skills, it is quite another to *develop* them. As discussed earlier, a number of companies have maintained competitive advantages by consistently maintaining superior skills and capabilities in their sales forces. Relationship-building skills are perhaps the most important set of skills that distinguish the best from the rest. These skills are acquired over the course of many years and are developed in unique ways, depending on the individual. Two general modes for developing relationship skills are:

1. First develop industry or applications expertise, and gradually

develop the interpersonal and business savvy required to perform the trusted-advisor role.

2. First develop general business diagnostics skills and apply them to provide on-the-spot guidance to customers. These individuals then augment their diagnostic skills with industry and application expertise to become full trusted advisors.

Some sales executives argue that it is better to start with industry or applications expertise, and develop the diagnostic skills over time. Others argue that they can't teach business diagnostic skills as well as they can teach industry or applications expertise, so they prefer to recruit only those individuals with proven capabilities in business diagnosis, and then they teach industry and applications expertise.

The truth of the matter is that there are no shortcuts to developing strong customer relationship management skills. Individuals achieve trusted-advisor status from either of the routes previously described, but individuals never achieve this stature overnight. Furthermore, since trusted advisorship is such a difficult role to achieve, companies should be open to either path. In many ways, the path to being a trusted advisor is a personal journey and cannot be broken down into a regimen. The important thing is to manage the development of relationship managers on an individualized basis. This is the best way to ensure that the company is constantly moving people through the stages of becoming trusted advisors.

COST AND PROFIT INFORMATION. Acquisition efforts need to be founded on the assumption that the team is involved in generating profit for the company. To make this assumption a reality, measures of projected cost and account profitability are needed, and engagement management as well as product costs need to be included in the formula.

Of particular relevance in the specification process is the cost of the resources assembled to win the business. Without any measurement and consequent responsibility for acquisition costs, team leaders are likely to overstaff their teams and overinvest in hard costs to maximize the likelihood of a win. Consequently, companies need to develop procedures for tracking the time and cost of the resources utilized during the specification phase.

Engagement team leaders also need to anticipate that they will be responsible for the actual, not just the planned, profit of the business they are seeking. This is especially important if the specification team turns the account over to an exchange manager.

CUSTOMER STUDY AND PROPOSAL FORMATS. Companies should collect examples of best practices for customer studies and value proposals, and then distribute them within the organization. These formats can be used as guidelines or inspiration for tailoring documents for specific prospects. Specification teams should always keep in mind that customers mentally compare them not just to their direct competitors, but also to the most impressive presentations the customer has ever witnessed.

DATABASES. Engagement managers need databases to track and share critical information about the pursuit of new business opportunities. To be effective, a number of individuals must "touch" an opportunity before it is converted into business. Previously, only one person had a complete history on the opportunity: the lead salesperson. Now, it is necessary to build an information system to retain a chronology of what has transpired with the prospect so that all involved are up to date with what has transpired during the engagement process. Some of the vital information that can be stored and distributed among the engagement team includes:

1. Names, titles, roles, contact record, history of previous engagement efforts

2. Planned activities, schedules of events, milestones

3. Progress-to-date, outcomes of key events, commitments made

COMMUNICATIONS. Communications also play a critical role in the effectiveness of the specification process. In addition to the need for the communications support described earlier under "Identification," studies and proposals need to be prepared for prospects. While formats are one step to ensuring quality, document preparation typically should be shared among several types of team members. For example, a team comprising a representative, analyst, and desktop specialist can be quite effective. Also, the engagement team must be able to communicate frequently, and technology, such as voice- and e-mail and teleconferencing, combined with good old-fashioned team meetings, becomes essential.

EXCHANGE

The primary objective of the exchange process is to deliver a profitable outcome for the customer and the company. Some critical activities in the exchange process include providing start-to-finish involvement; assessment and redesign, customized production, delivery, and installation; responsive problem solving; and customer training and education. We also review some important exchange support tools.

START-TO-FINISH INVOLVEMENT

During the exchange process, the firm has two objectives: fully delivering the promise to the customer and ensuring that the customer appropriately reimburses the supplier for value received. While the leader of the specification effort will remain involved for some time after the supplier starts to deliver, it is more and more common for customers to expect that responsibility for the relationship will be shared among other customer-coverage personnel and managers. By the same token, other companies are more effective at delivering promised value to the customer or collecting on what is due when the team leader stays with the customer through the entire life cycle of the relationship.

Some companies argue that it is essential to hand off responsibility for managing the exchange. Top-notch specification team leaders are so rare and have such a high market value and economic impact on the company that they must be transitioned out of the exchange process and moved on to focus on the next business opportunity.

But what if the next best business opportunity is with the same customer? And what about the economic impact of invoices paid in full and on time? What about testimonials from the satisfied customer that can be used as references to generate additional new business? What about ensuring that the anticipated profitability of the deal actually materializes for the supplier as well as for the customer?

These considerations can provide a compelling case for end-to-end engagement management responsibility. This is not to say that end-to-end responsibility is for every company. We are saying, however, that too often companies assume that responsibility for exchange should be transferred to other parts of the company rather than retained by those individuals who managed the identification and specification processes. In making the transfer, the risk of exchange failure may increase, consequently limiting future strategic and economic opportunities.

An example of a company that used the start-to-finish approach with its sales force is R. R. Donnelley. The Donnelley way included a promise to their customers that the salesperson would stay with them through the entire printing process. Donnelley would be at the plant when direct-mail catalogs came off the line and were being shipped to make sure that Donnelley's promise to the customer was being fulfilled. This approach was used as a point of strategic differentiation by Donnelley. Other companies did not keep the salesperson in the customer relationship management process from start to finish, and Donnelley took advantage of this. To effectively execute this approach, the salesperson training process was substantially longer and more involved, but Donnelley proved over many years that there was a significant payoff.

ASSESSMENT AND REDESIGN

Assessment consists primarily of comparing the value proposal with reality. During the implementation of the proposal, there are bound to be surprises, as dictated by Murphy's Law. If responsibility for tracking nonconformance with the proposal is completely delegated to the customer's purchasing function, the supplier surrenders control over the long-term relationship. Since this is a shortsighted and costly mistake, suppliers must partner with their customers to assess the impact of the purchase. This approach also helps to maintain barriers to competitive entry because it reduces the likelihood of dissatisfied customers contacting other competitive suppliers.

Customers assess the value of a supplier's total product offering by determining how much wealth creation will result for them. This calculation of revenue improvement potential considers the technology, design features, and zero-defect reliability of the product. Customers also determine the potential cost savings: materials handling, working-capital requirements, production efficiencies, ongoing operational or maintenance costs, and/or the amount of scrap or defects.

Formally or informally, the customer subtracts the total cost of the supplier's offering from its calculation of the offering's total value. The total cost of dealing with a particular supplier for a specific product includes external costs—the product price, freight, insurance—plus the customer's internal costs for using that supplier—negotiations, invoicing, communications, logistical capabilities, and training.

It is critical that information is gathered from the assessment and is used to do two things. First, the value proposal needs to be recalibrated based on this new information. The recalibration can lead to any number of follow-up steps, including redesign of the current solution to make it more effective. Feedback on implementation effectiveness helps the company develop improved solutions that can be implemented either as part of the original proposal or as additional work. Second, feedback on the experience should be channeled back into the identification and specification processes. This helps to ensure that what works is repeated and that errors in prospect identification or customer specification are corrected in future efforts.

Customized Production, Delivery, and Installation

With the intense degree of customization required for success in today's procurement world, the number of times a company can merely ship products by order number is declining quickly. Instead, exchange teams are required to produce, deliver, and install customized solutions to customer problems. While stock products may be shipped, the total product offering must provide a solution to the customer, and solutions usually do not come in boxes.

Responsive Problem Solving

Not only do problems need to be solved, but solutions need to appear quickly. Ongoing team responsibilities need to be assigned so that the customer has multiple avenues available to voice concerns, and the company needs to have coordinated and focused corrective procedures in place. Problem solving can also entail conducting an assessment of other exchange activities to find answers to problems. Or earlier outcomes of the engagement process may need to be reassessed; sometimes the specification was inaccurate or the wrong solution was arrived at.

Customer Training and Education

The goal of training and education is to transfer a sufficient amount of knowledge to the customer so that the benefits promised in the proposal can be achieved. Customers may not know how to solve their problems; providing solutions is part of the value being delivered by the supplier. Consequently, the supplier must educate the customer on how to keep the newly installed solution working. If the education is not viewed as an integral part of the implementation, then customer satisfaction and the likelihood of a rebuy are likely to suffer due to failure to perform as promised. To say it was the customer's fault is not sufficient; it should be expected that the customer will not succeed unless educated in solution maintenance.

SUPPORT TOOLS FOR THE EXCHANGE PROCESS

Some tools that can enhance the effectiveness of the exchange process include execution plans, performance measures and rewards, and information systems.

EXECUTION PLANS.   Postsale implementation performance is often lost in the first thrill of victory. The customer agreed to buy, so off the firm goes to the next opportunity. Customers, however, do not view a sale as a sale until they are satisfied with the purchase. To ensure their satisfaction, a plan for ensuring the full implementation of the value proposal is needed. Tasks need to be specified along with associated responsibilities and time frames. Common plan elements include production, testing, delivery, installation, training, and service.

PERFORMANCE MEASURES AND REWARDS.   Many firms now question short-term, transaction-oriented performance measures and rewards. Measuring and rewarding salespeople for unit volume, gross margin per sales, and gross margin per product does not fully capture success during the exchange process. Instead, companies are exploring new measures like order accuracy, fill rate, response time, customer satisfaction, cycle time, and defect rate. Furthermore, these new measures gradually are being incorporated into rewards for the entire engagement team, as well as for the salesperson.

INFORMATION SYSTEMS.   Information systems must better enable companies to measure relevant performance and to distribute information to their front-line personnel. The information systems also must be able to mirror the decision processes the company wants followed so that engagement team members have the information they need. As information systems evolve over the next decade, more engagement teams will be able to grapple with the ultimate measures of firm success: customer goodwill and customer profitability.

Many firms have invested in sales-force automation hardware, but two pieces are still missing. First, the source information is not adequate enough to provide effective customer intelligence. Second, the protocols for how to handle the information are not well developed. Our surveys indicate that many sales and engagement team members average up to 50 faxes or voicemail entries each day.

The problem with this kind of one-way communication is that the sender assumes that the recipient has the information and mentally signs off on the information as having been successfully transmitted. The net result is that order errors can be very high—for example, when purchasers fax in an order and assume that it is then complete and ready for fulfillment. In too many cases, suppliers do not designate the protocols for what information has to be in the fax and the procedures for internally transferring the information to the right people. The customer's expectation of speedy response is not only missed but the error rate is unexpectedly high.

Many sales automation efforts have focused on placing hardware in the hands of salespeople, but there is often insufficient communication with the information systems professionals who are responsible for providing information. A lot of current sales automation software is just a variation of traditional time and territory management tools. Sales automation may make people more efficient, but it does not address core information technology issues in ways that make engagement teams more effective. Voicemail, e-mail, laptop computers, and EDI (electronic data interchange) systems may make possible a high volume of customer transactions, but they do not support either adequate customer communications or improved decision making around customer requests.

Like every other aspect of selling, communication technology has to be continually adjusted to support the exchange process and to provide the basis for continuous improvement. The engagement team must be able to bring in bits of customer information and then transmit this information throughout the organization so that appropriate action can be taken.

As firms move away from simple selling transactions and toward more complex exchanges, information systems must change to meet a very different set of needs. Most importantly, systems will have to track indicators of progress in building long-term customer relationships and calculate the ROI and profitability consequences which occur when there are customer-by-customer variations in the product offering. For most firms, their current information and communication systems are just a starting place to record, communicate, and process the information engagement teams need to be more effective.

CONCLUSION

In this chapter, we have reviewed how the power shift and the consequent failures in sales and marketing have left many companies stranded in a bygone era. These companies need to drop their dependence on functions and mass marketing, and aggressively explore the tremendous potential of the engagement process. Once the full range of engagement options is well understood, a company is ready to develop its engagement strategy, a step that is explored in the next chapter.

ENGAGEMENT STRATEGY

The next tool we would like to explore is engagement strategy. In this chapter we outline how companies can define the three core components of engagement—position, execution, and cost—and then develop an engagement strategy that will guide their reengineering efforts. The work required to develop an engagement strategy involves a lot of technical detail, which is addressed in this chapter.

POSITION

Companies need to understand the full range of options for adding value to the customer before they can define their engagement positions. The range of value-added options constitutes what we refer to as a *position hierarchy*. In other words, the position hierarchy is a spectrum of options currently used or potentially usable for completing the engagement process. The following steps are useful for defining a company's position.

1. *Construct a position hierarchy.* Each company needs to define hierarchies that correspond to its unique businesses. Examples of hierarchies for the three phases of the engagement process are provided in Figures 7-1 through 7-3.

When developing a position hierarchy, it is important to identify opportunities for adding value that go beyond, as well as below, the company's current position. Most industries

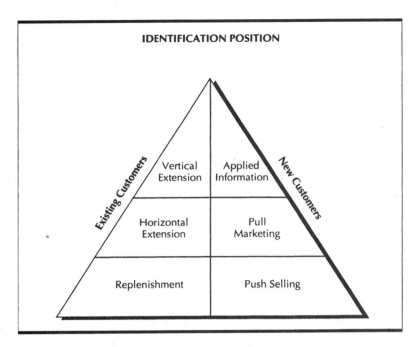

IDENTIFICATION POSITION

Existing Customers | New Customers

Vertical Extension | Applied Information

Horizontal Extension | Pull Marketing

Replenishment | Push Selling

Figure 7-1 *Position hierarchy for the identification process.*

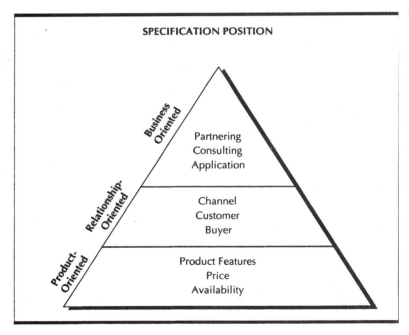

SPECIFICATION POSITION

Business Oriented

Partnering
Consulting
Application

Relationship- Oriented

Channel
Customer
Buyer

Product- Oriented

Product Features
Price
Availability

Figure 7-2 *Position hierarchy for the specification process.*

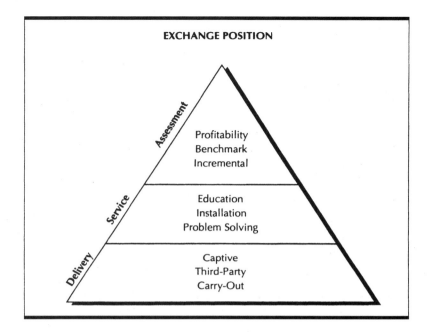

EXCHANGE POSITION

Assessment

Profitability
Benchmark
Incremental

Service

Education
Installation
Problem Solving

Delivery

Captive
Third-Party
Carry-Out

Figure 7-3   *Position hierarchy for the exchange process.*

have a number of distribution channels and other options for engaging with customers. These various approaches constitute the hierarchy of available options for the company.

2. *Identify the company's position.*   The company's position within the hierarchy needs to be established. Companies sometimes emphasize the exception when they describe their positions; this is not as useful as honestly describing how the company typically conducts the engagement process. Surveys and interviews with customers can be quite useful in making accurate assessments of a company's true position. It also may be helpful to identify different company positions for different customer groups, such as global, national, and geographic accounts.

EXECUTION

Execution refers to how well a particular position is performed. Referring to Chapter 5, remember that, even though P&G adopted an average position, they delivered more value than the competition because they had above-average execution. A company defines its execution by taking the following steps:

1. *Identify the company's position.* This step is completed when defining position. The implication here is that you cannot define execution without first establishing a position to assess.

2. *Develop relevant assessment criteria.* Figures 7-4 through 7-6 provide illustrative assessment criteria for the identification, specification, and exchange processes. Assessment criteria need to be tailored to the company's position. For example, if a company has a low-value position, then its assessment criteria should focus on the dimensions of performance relevant for that low-value position.

Position	Execution Assessment Criteria
IDENTIFICATION ASSESSMENT	
Existing Customers	
◆ Vertical Extension	• Effective leverage of prior experience to identify larger issue
	• Appropriate match between opportunity and supplier resources
◆ Horizontal Extension	• Appropriate use of customer contacts to identify next opportunity
	• Appropriate timing to pursue the opportunity
	• Degree of fit between current and targeted application
◆ Replenishment	• Ease and speed of order entry
	• Availability of one-stop shopping
New Customers	
◆ Applied Information	• New insights were obtained by applying supplier's industry information or diagnostic tools
◆ Pull Marketing	• New business leads are generated by marketing expenditures
	• Leads are qualified and match the company's target customer profile
◆ Push Selling	• Efficient description of company capabilities
	• Appropriate use of salesperson's contacts and network to gain appointment

Figure 7-4

SPECIFICATION ASSESSMENT	
Position	**Execution Assessment Criteria**
Business-Oriented	
◆ Partnering	• A willingness to conduct business in entirely new ways was demonstrated
	• True customer/supplier synergies were identified in the proposal
◆ Consulting	• New insights into our business were provided
	• Significant performance improvement opportunities were identified
◆ Application	• The issue was defined accurately
	• A strong business case was prepared, including financial pro formas
Relationship-Oriented	
◆ Channel	• Distribution channel opinions were consulted and integrated into the specifications
◆ Customer	• End-user needs were accurately identified
	• Appropriate customer representatives were consulted to develop final specifications
◆ Buyer	• All required specification steps were completed
	• All specification steps were completed on time
Product-Oriented	
◆ Product Features	• The products' features were accurately described
	• The features described were aligned with the customer's business
◆ Price	• A fair price was quoted
	• Available discounts were given
◆ Availability	• An accurate description of availability was provided

Figure 7-5

Also, assessment criteria need to encompass execution of lower-level positions as well as the company's target position. For example, if a company targets vertical extensions, it should also assess how well it performs horizontal extensions and replenishment.

3. *Conduct the assessment.* There are a variety of ways to conduct an assessment, and companies need to find which methods are relevant for their situation. For example, an objective assessment can be conducted by management, assessment surveys can be mailed to customers, focus groups can be held with customers, or personal interviews with customers can be conducted.

	EXCHANGE ASSESSMENT	
Position	**Execution Assessment Criteria**	
Assessment-Oriented		
◆ Profitability	• A thorough understanding of profit implications was demonstrated	
	• A thorough review of the project's impact was assessed	
◆ Benchmark	• Relevant benchmarks were used to assess performance	
◆ Incremental	• A review of contractual obligation fulfillment was conducted	
	• Actual results were compared to historical performance levels	
Service-Oriented		
◆ Education	• Critical knowledge was transferred to relevant parties	
	• Relevant customer parties are capable of full maintenance of the new application	
◆ Installation	• Installation was completed on time and on budget	
	• Customer staff was effectively used during the installation	
◆ Problem Solving	• Issues were identified early or before they had a negative impact on operations	
	• Responses to problems were quick and effective	
Delivery-Oriented		
◆ Captive	• Delivery personnel were helpful in placement of shipments	
◆ Third-Party	• Delivery was on time and per instructions	
	• Shipping charges were competitive	
◆ Carry-Out	• Supplier flexibly allowed us pickup upon request	

Figure 7-6

COST

The cost component of the engagement equation is different from traditional cost numbers, since it is defined relative to competition. Traditionally, companies generate rich data on departmental operating costs, and some companies have the ability to allocate these costs to customers or transactions. While useful for day-to-day management and control purposes, costs without benchmarks have limited strategic use. Under the engagement equation, each component, including cost, is benchmarked against competition. The following steps are useful in acquiring engagement cost numbers that can be compared to those of competitors:

1. *Define engagement expense.* Focus where competitor data is available. For example, sales compensation is typically the

major component of engagement expenses, and pay surveys defining industry norms are frequently available. Expanding on this concept, field organization headcounts of competitors, combined with average pay levels for these same field positions, can be obtained through custom industry surveys.

2. *Define engagement outcome.* Following the same rule of competitor comparisons, sales revenue is frequently the best engagement outcome to track. While profit-related numbers, such as gross margin dollars per customer, are important for other strategic analyses, they have limited usefulness here because competitors frequently will not share profit-related information.

3. *Calculate cost of engagement.* Dividing of engagement expense by engagement outcome creates a cost ratio that allows a company to compare itself with the competition or the industry.

To arrive at the cost for identification, acquisition, and exchange, companies must estimate how much time various functions spend on each process. Then, they can then apportion to each process its share of the average total compensation paid to the involved functions. For example, if a company determines that it devotes one-third of the average salesperson's time to identification, and average total annual compensation is $100,000 per salesperson, a company with 100 salespeople and 1000 customers is spending $3.3 million a year on identification, or $3300 per customer per year. These costs must be viewed relative to the costs incurred by key competitors. If the analysis reveals that competitors are spending far less or far more on a specific process, the company can begin to build a real understanding of its competitive status and what it will take to change it.

Most firms already have information about total compensation paid by competitors. Getting information about the amount of time competitors devote to each of the three processes may be more difficult, but many firms can get this information from employees they have hired from competitor firms, and from surveys. In some cases, the information may be anecdotal, or it may be the firm's best estimate of competitors' practices.

FUTURE ENGAGEMENT STRATEGY MEASURES

The preceding approach to measuring position, execution, and cost is comparative; all three components were defined relative to the competition. We have recommended this approach because it is very difficult for companies to define their *actual* return on engagement expenditures. A reliable engagement return measure would require a precise definition of the premium customers pay for engagement value, or a precise measure of the incremental sales generated by the engagement process. Usually, companies can only make rough estimates of this premium. Or, they find that customers do not actually pay a premium for engagement value added, but that critical ratios, such as lead-to-sale conversion or customer retention, improve as engagement value increases. In the future, companies may be better able to define the economic value of engagement. Until then, engagement strategy formulation exercises need to focus on measures that have competitive benchmarks.

ENGAGEMENT STRATEGY

Once a company has defined its position, execution, and cost relative to the competition, it is then possible to examine strategic alternatives for improving engagement process contribution. In this section, we first will establish a base case for a company in financial services, then we will examine several strategic options for the company.

BASE CASE

The company described in Figure 7-7 had a unique approach to managing the specification process. Its position was to add significant value to prospects by providing them with financial guidance, in addition to recommending appropriate investment products. The philosophy was to use this value added as a way to increase the company's close rate and ultimately gain a greater share of the customer's assets that could be used for investment purposes.

While the company had an excellent specification concept, its execution was not impressive enough to create a large gap between itself and competitors. Furthermore, this company's sales force productivity was very low relative to its specification costs. It was spending a lot of money to train salespeople on the unique concept, but these salespeople were turning over to other companies who valued their training and would pay them more. Consequently, the company's production was below average. The company also had some difficulties with its client services; too often responses to client service requests were slow or inaccurate.

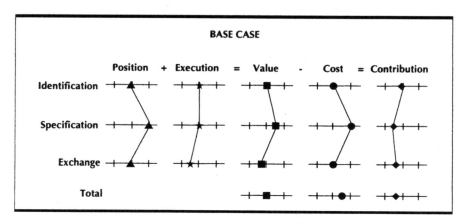

Figure 7-7 *Base-case example of a financial services company.*

COMPETITIVENESS

One reengineering strategy for this financial services company was to reestablish competitiveness. This could be done by focusing on the value or the cost side of identification, specification, or execution. Figure 7-8 illustrates how this company could focus on specification to establish competitiveness. By improving the execution of its specification strategy, it could improve value added to customers, increase its prospect-to-client conversion rate, and improve productivity.

During its reengineering study, this company found that a comprehensive set of changes involving recruiting, selection, training, development, systems enhancements, and field support were needed to achieve a noticeable improvement in specification execution, and associated productivity improvements would not follow for several years. Therefore, if it only wanted to achieve competitiveness, its chances of success were greater if it lowered its specification position, cut the associated high costs for executing this high position, and fixed its exchange execution problems.

The other major option for establishing competitiveness was

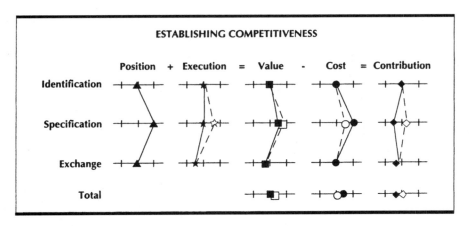

Figure 7-8 *The financial services company focuses on specification to establish competitiveness.*

to embrace higher positions. Many companies adopt high positions because they believe that this will push them toward higher returns. But if execution remains average, the move to a higher position will not create a significant jump in returns.

LEADERSHIP

Given the unattractiveness of the competitiveness options, this financial services company explored the requirements for gaining a leadership position. One primary option was examined: across-the-board execution improvements, as illustrated in Figure 7-9. Such a strategy would greatly increase the value added to customers, thereby increasing customer satisfaction, retention, and sales productivity.

As the company investigated what it would take to dramatically distinguish its execution from that of competitors, it found that a broad array of human resource management, support, and systems enhancements would be required. Again, productivity improvements would not offset execution enhancement investments for at least several years, and there would be several other competitors with more effective field organizations.

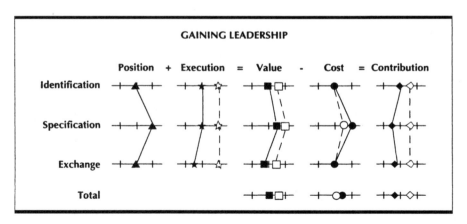

Figure 7-9 *Across-the-board execution improvements to gain a leadership position.*

This company did not seriously consider a cost reduction approach to achieving leadership. Its overall profitability was strong, and the below-market field contribution could be tolerated while improvements were made. The company further reasoned that their high identification position would probably need to be abandoned with a low-cost leadership strategy.

QUANTUM LEAP

Given the substantial amount of effort, time, and expenditure required to execute the leadership strategy, this company also wanted to examine what would be required to achieve a quantum leap and establish itself as the top-performing company in the industry. As illustrated in Figure 7-10, the company would craft a long-term vision of radically improved position and execution. It would identify top positions throughout the engagement process and execute them with distinction. While the company would invest far more than competitors would on its field organization, these expenditures would be offset by high sales per person in the field organization.

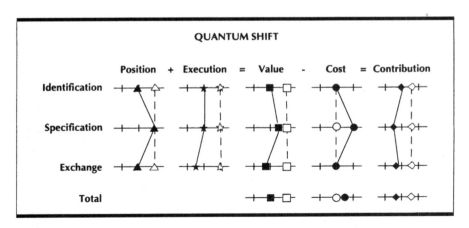

Figure 7-10 *A quantum shift in position and execution to become the top-performing company.*

Valley of Despair

The quantum leap/radical departure strategy is motivated by the realization that considerable effort has been expended in trying to establish leadership, yet other companies remain superior. This is a strong argument in favor of the quantum leap. However, the intervening period of time until the quantum leap is fully carried out may carry little contribution improvement for the company, as illustrated in Figure 7-11. Execution of the high position may be below competitive standards for a period of time, and productivity may be slow to materialize. This "valley of despair" that a company traverses en route to implementing a quantum leap can be very costly to a company.

Many companies adopt a high position because they believe that this will push them toward higher returns. But if execution remains average, the move to a higher position will not create a dramatic jump in returns. Understanding this is really nothing more than applying systems thinking—it is the interaction or the relationship among position, execution, and costs that is crucial in the push for greater returns. No single element can produce

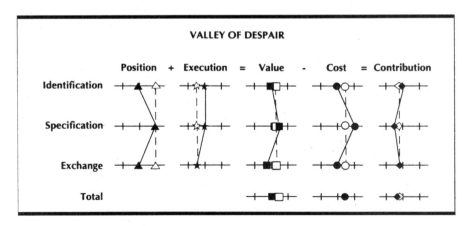

Figure 7-11 *The time interval before completion of the quantum leap may yield little improvement and may constitute a "valley of despair."*

significantly greater returns if the other elements are not geared to the same result.

To manage quantum-leap risks, companies frequently test their quantum-shift concepts to gauge the length of time required to implement them and the intervening impact on execution effectiveness and cost. While companies can become very enthused with the potential of the quantum leap, the realities of implementation must also be squarely confronted.

COST STRATEGIES

It is also possible to make radical leaps by using a cost strategy, as illustrated in Figure 7-12. A company like Dell, or a new retail format, like warehouse stores, is reflected here, where a new channel of, or approach to, distribution is designed to deliver extremely well on a low position. This figure also reflects the strategy adopted by IBM Series/1. Note that some companies use a dramatic cost strategy as a vehicle to transfer savings to customers in the form of lower prices.

A less dramatic cost strategy example was reviewed in Chapter 5: the Carnation Company before it was acquired by Nestlé. Carnation maintained its sales force at costs that were

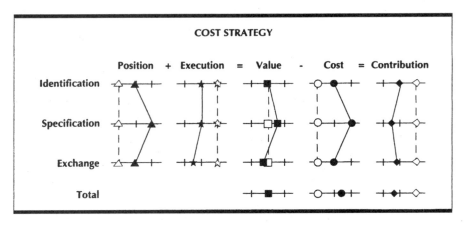

Figure 7-12 *Making a quantum leap by using a cost strategy.*

structurally lower than those of the competition for servicing and selling at grocery stores. Because its direct sales compensation was relatively low, Carnation's turnover was higher than average. To execute its cost strategy, a below-market pay strategy, combined with above-average benefits, resulted in a significant cost advantage for Carnation year after year. The cost of the above-average benefits was not nearly as much as the advantage gained from below-market compensation. By recruiting good students with team sports backgrounds from middle-tier colleges, Carnation was able to maintain a homogeneous and team-oriented sales force, and pay below market. This approach was a direct contrast to the P&G recruiting strategy of drawing from top-tier schools.

To further support its low-pay approach, Carnation had an unwritten rule of not discussing pay. The story is told that, when you received a promotion at Carnation, you said "thank you" and waited for your paycheck to see how much of an increase you received. This low-pay-prominence philosophy was very effective in helping the company maintain a significant cost advantage relative to competitors.

FOUR LESSONS

From the companies we have worked with, we have gathered four important lessons for selecting the right reengineering strategy, developing realistic expectations, and ensuring a successful outcome:

1. *Understand the difficulty of change and select a strategy that will help the firm cope with it.* A company looking for a high position or shooting for high execution will not get there overnight. If the company is spending money in its attempt to get there, its return will probably drop in the short term. In other words, things may get worse before they get better. This is the "valley of despair" that is so tortuous. The company will

begin to pull out of it when employees begin to turn around and execution starts to rise from average to above average to excellent. Most quantum-shift strategies involve a valley of despair; a company must anticipate them and be able to weather them financially. Otherwise, the company will abandon the new strategy before the change effort has run its course.

2. *Concentrate on the relationship and the balance between the three highly interdependent components of position, execution, and cost.* The problem with most change efforts is that they focus on position or execution or cost, but fail to look at the relationships among the three and their impact on returns. Although the close link between execution and costs is usually clear, the link between position and costs, while also close, is often less obvious.

   A common scenario is for a company to adopt bold ideas that put it into a high position, but then to drop the ball on execution while at the same time incurring high cost. Execution failures are commonplace; that is why Lou Gerstner of IBM stresses that "strategy is execution." When execution and costs are not balanced, the company is in trouble.

   It is also important to stay alert for interactions between engagement strategy and the core product. For example, Dell used its engagement cost strategy to cut computer prices.

3. *Investigate the full spectrum of strategy and outcome alternatives.* A common problem with change efforts is that they assume that up is better: a higher position is a better position, and better execution is always more competitive. In fact, up is not always better, and a company must be free to look at all the options—higher and lower, more and less—before it can select the right strategy for its specific competitive situation and for optimal returns.

   Focusing on one process to the exclusion of others can become a dangerous habit. One company we worked with, for example, had a high identification and acquisition position and a low exchange position. Its execution was average to slightly above average. Out of sheer force of habit and culture, the company remained focused on identification and acquisition long after its industry had reached a mature stage of development requiring low costs and highly efficient exchange.

4. *Focus on the right selling process.* The three selling processes—identification, acquisition, and exchange—are not of equal importance in all firms or in all industries. Also, they do not have equal costs. In some firms, acquisition costs are higher than exchange costs. But in other firms, exchange involves systems and huge expenditures for technology and communications.

Given the trend for procurement to favor a smaller number of suppliers, acquisition will become an increasingly important and expensive process. Exchange will become more critical because that's where suppliers can lose the customers that will cost them so much to get back. Sales forces are reluctant to move into exchange because they think it diminishes their power, when, in fact, it is the only way for them to *preserve* their power in the long run.

THREE

TOOLS

A host of new tools is required to implement new engagement strategies. Even great strategies are worthless without execution, and the management tools of the old selling and marketing eras are often ineffective as, if not actually contradictory to, the drivers of success in the new engagement era. This section of the book helps companies begin the daunting task of retooling so that they can implement their new engagement strategies.

CHAPTER	SUMMARY
8 Measuring Return and Effectiveness	In the new engagement era, it is critical to measure enduring return on customer relationships. This happens in two ways. First, the outputs of the engagement process are measured and evaluated. Second, the effectiveness of the process is measured. In this chapter we also address issues such as measuring individual contributions in a team environment, measuring and paying for customer satisfaction, and introducing new performance measures without creating unwanted disruptions.
9 Developing Early Warning Systems	When must a firm attempt a quantum-leap improvement in performance? What are the macrolevel indicators of whether the current engagement process is working? This chapter provides a guide for how companies can answer these questions and develop an "early warning system" in time to avoid the need for a massive and disruptive change effort all at once.

(Continued)

CHAPTER	SUMMARY
10 The Reengineering Process	First-generation reengineering efforts have largely avoided redesigning the sales and marketing processes. Also, the reengineering process itself needs to be reengineered to increase its cycle time and its overall success rate. This chapter demonstrates how to modify the reengineering process to match each company's unique needs and to enhance the chances of successful national rollouts of redesigned sales and marketing processes.
11 Forming and Leading Teams	To bring the company to the customer, effective teams become crucial. What are the differences between teamwork and teams? How do you help teams be successful? How do you clarify roles and set performance goals? How do you reward teams? These and related questions are addressed in this chapter.
12 Contracting with Employees	Translating strategic change and reengineered processes into clear individual contributions is a critical step in executing a reengineering effort. In this chapter we explore performance contracts, and how managers need to spend their own time and expand their people development and educational efforts. We also provide an analytical framework to help companies gauge how much change can be introduced without unduly jeopardizing their chances of success.

MEASURING RETURN AND EFFECTIVENESS

What are the financial consequences of missing the exchange demands of your best customer? How does a supplier recapture the cost of the investment it takes to have competitively differentiated executional mastery? How can a supplier measure the value of a loyal customer? Few sales executives would argue that thriving in the next decade requires taking actions every year which build improved profitability and productivity. Meeting evolving new customer needs and procurement capabilities requires examining in finer detail not only a firm's cost structure and pricing strategies, but also its process-by-process effectiveness at engaging customers. Monitoring progress requires measuring the stability of the firm's customer base and the value of the goodwill accrued from customers. Indicators of customer-base stability and goodwill are also necessary for evaluating the risks and opportunities of the firm.

This chapter delineates the challenges facing the firm's financial analysts, cost accountants, and information systems experts who must shift their focus from measuring product, asset, and production profitability to the necessity of creating information and accounting systems which are built on the stream of costs and profits that flow from customer engagements.

Our objective here is to outline the conceptual parameters of meeting the challenge of building for that new accounting and management information systems capability. To meet this objective, we must first describe a new measure of the contributions which result from a successful engagement process...or the enduring return from successful customer relationships.

MEASURING ENDURING RETURN

As we have seen in earlier chapters, procurement capabilities are changing in ways which will significantly alter how suppliers invest in finding, acquiring, and sustaining customer relationships.

Taking a series of "snapshots" over time to determine whether a firm is building or jeopardizing its investment in improving its customer relationships requires examining both the financial and nonfinancial transactions of the engagement process. To have a *long-lasting or enduring* customer relationship, a supplier must continually meet the customer's demands for quality, responsiveness, service, knowledge, JIT delivery, product redesign, and so on. To ensure a stream of return or profits from their customer relationships, suppliers must not only price their core products competitively but also capture a premium for the value added during the engagement process. To gain enduring return from a customer relationship, a supplier must not only capture the value (or price) of both the core product offering and the value added during the engagement process, but the supplier also must build the switch-out costs of the relationship so high that the barriers to competitors are prohibitive. Figure 8-1 summarizes some of the indicators which could be used to calculate how well the firm is building its level of enduring return with a customer.

As present trends continue, many customers' procurement strategies will call for fewer but longer-lasting relationships with suppliers. If suppliers wish to be retained by these customers both now and for the long haul, it is essential that they build for endurance as well as for profitability or return.

Measure	To Gain This Measure, A Supplier Must:
An enduring customer relationship	Meet customer demand for: ◆ Quality ◆ Responsiveness ◆ Service ◆ Knowledge ◆ JIT delivery ◆ Product redesign
Contribution from the customer relationship	◆ Price core products competitively ◆ Capture engagement process value added in additional pricing premium
Enduring return from the customer relationship	◆ Capture value of core product offering ◆ Capture value added during engagement process ◆ Build relationship value to high level so switch-out costs are prohibitive

Figure 8-1 *Indicators of enduring return.*

Currently, the set of indicators many firms use to ascertain whether they are building or diluting their enduring return is incomplete. Although most suppliers have well-established procedures for measuring the costs represented in their core product offerings, few suppliers have developed procedures for measuring either their costs of or the value delivered during the engagement process. The cost accounting systems of most firms are incapable of providing this information to managers.

Accounting science currently calculates profitability by building on rules for allocating assets, expenses, and revenues by function or department. Firms allocate this data to measure profitability by product line. To move beyond product profitability to measuring profitability by customer requires a major leap in capability for most accounting systems.

Measuring enduring return from the firm's engagement activities requires more than a snapshot; an analysis of these indicators must be conducted over a period of time. To be truly incisive, the analysis should be done for each account in that 20 to 30 percent of the customer base which represents 70 to 80 percent of the firm's revenues or profits.

Why Is Enduring Return Important?

To some extent, the concept of enduring return is currently measured in some accounting valuation procedures under the title of goodwill. In the same fashion that a company depreciates capital equipment, a supplier needs a way to measure the net present value of customer goodwill, given that the supplier will invest its information systems, its technical skills, and its reengineered capabilities to build relationships with customers.

As firms become more aware of the importance of enduring customer relationships, fuller development of how to calculate goodwill becomes more important, as it needs to be used to measure a firm's capacity to make informed investment decisions.

The evolving tendency of customers to demand that the supplier's organization reengineer the way work is performed entails risks and high costs. At a time when most firms require that typical capital equipment investment requests have a payback time frame of anywhere from two to five years in order for the request to be approved, undertaking a decision to invest in various customer relationships requires considering similar investment and payback time frames.

As more and more suppliers need to differentiate how they distribute their products or services, suppliers must be able to approximate ROI on a customer-by-customer basis. And it is not possible to measure the potential ROI from decisions about customers until the enduring return from each major customer can be projected.

MEASURING ENGAGEMENT PROCESS EFFECTIVENESS

In a traditional and functionally organized firm, the performance of salespersons, sales offices, and, to an extent, the entire sales function, can be measured according to ratios such as these:

- Sales dollars per hour = gross sales ÷ total hours worked
- Sales per person = number of sales ÷ number of salespeople
- Sales dollars per salesperson = gross sales ÷ number of salespeople
- Average dollars per sale = gross sales in dollars ÷ number of transactions

These ratios can help companies identify outstanding and substandard relative financial performance. The key words, however, are *relative* and *financial*. The ratios demonstrate efficiency but don't show the whole picture, only a part. However, managers take them as the whole truth, when they are only partial. If the appropriate data were available, it would be possible to compare the impact of the supplier's performance on the firm's customers with that of competitors. For example, an MRO (maintenance, repair, and operations) distributor routinely compares its dollar sales per employee with figures for the entire industry. These figures are published by an association that collects data from all its members. These ratios are almost completely financially focused; they are useful only to managers who want to compare financial performances within the industry. Nevertheless, these ratios are universally used, and a great deal of significance is drawn from them. We suggest that firms must also measure performance through a series of internal and external indicators which measure the effectiveness of the firm's engagement processes.

INTERNAL INDICATORS

As Figure 8-2 summarizes, suppliers can assess their effectiveness through each phase of the engagement process. Completing an assessment of effectiveness requires reviewing not only the hard data indicators of results but also the adequacy of the support tools which indicate that personnel are, or are not, performing effectively.

Process Phase	Input Indicators	Support Tools
Prospect Identification	◆ Percent of potential customers in target markets ◆ Lead-to-proposal rate ◆ Percent of customers to whom firm has become a top contender	◆ Adherence to prospect identification process ◆ Quality of leads and prospects: fit with target markets, profit potential of leads
Customer Acquisition	◆ Lead-to-close, proposal-to-close rates ◆ Percent top-supplier reputation among customers ◆ Percent of no-compete bids	◆ Adherence to customer acquisition strategy ◆ Quality of customer studies, proposals, trials, communications
Value Exchange	◆ Profitable customers ◆ Customer satisfaction levels ◆ Rebuy rate ◆ Percent of customers where firm has reached top-supplier status	◆ Quality of implementation plans ◆ Adherence to implementation plans ◆ Adherence to exchange strategy

Figure 8-2   *Assessing engagement process effectiveness.*

Conducting an examination rigorous enough to gain true insight into where improvements can be made may require a team from various functions of the organization. But an internal examination, although valuable, may not produce enough information to justify a major change effort. To complete any analysis of a firm's effectiveness with customers, some external studies must be initiated.

EXTERNAL INDICATORS

The way to sharpen the firm's assessment of its effectiveness is through examining practices of competitors. For each competitor, the assessment should determine its sales strategy, channel configuration, coverage, selling approach, improvement opportunities, process requirements, and reputation for quality. In addition to direct competitors, the assessment should include similar companies in related industries and best-in-class practitioners.

Failure to benchmark against the competition can jeopardize the financial health of any business. Xerox is a recent example. When foreign competitors eroded the imposing market share the company held during the 1970s and early 1980s, the CEO announced, "We had taken our eyes off the customer." He was right. For example, Xerox salespeople reported many times to design engineers that end-user customers complained about the inability of Xerox copiers to copy blue ink. The reply, "Tell customers to use black ink," branded Xerox as insensitive to customer needs and seriously eroded the company's competitive position.

Xerox began a strong change effort based on customer needs. Xerox also began benchmarking against competitors and the best in various business processes or functions, regardless of industry. These changes resulted in:

- A drop in defect rates from 8 percent to .03 percent
- An increase in return on investment from 8 percent of sales in 1986 to 14.2 percent in 1991
- A 20 percent increase in revenue per employee, and a corresponding decrease in manufacturing cost
- The company repositioning itself to think of competitors as a target from which market share could be *regained*

MEASURING PERSONAL CONTRIBUTIONS

Probably the first computerized system in most firms was order entry: quantity and model number. Since the first computer systems were built off shipment and invoice requests, it was common to measure customer value by adding all the invoices to calculate sales volume. Throughout the 1980s, more and more firms improved their capability to measure value by calculating both sales volume and the margin contribution of customers and sales reps.

Other firms pushed their approach toward measuring value even further. One firm in our Sales Force 2000 seminars calculates a salesperson's training costs, T&E, costs for the office, administrative costs, and costs for sales specialists and collateral material. The firm offsets these fully loaded sales support costs against the margin contribution of the responsible salesperson. The firm assumes that each salesperson is a minibusiness of his or her own, for which the firm measures margin contribution against its costs. In this case, the firm rewards the salesperson for maximizing the difference between margin contribution and costs. This approach represents a closer step to the kind of performance-measurement procedures firms will have to use in the next decade.

The next decade will also see firms looking for new ways to measure how each person contributes to building an enduring return from the customer base. Also, the labor value of the contribution assigned to different positions in the functional world—positions which were formerly involved in separate sales, service, and delivery departments—will have to be recast into a forward-looking world where people work in a process rather than a function and where each person may, in fact, bring a different and nontraditional value to the customer base.

Suppliers need a new methodology for determining the competitive market price of these jobs. The current thinking methods of determining the internal worth of jobs will change. For example, how integral is the customer service clerk? If the customer tells the supplier that it is the clerk who keeps the customer coming back, how can the supplier reward that clerk for effectiveness at retaining customers? The growing trend to include all customer-coverage positions on teams will accelerate not only the downward revaluing of sales jobs, but perhaps also the upward revaluation of all customer-coverage jobs.

Firms have started to move beyond a reliance on the short-term financial transaction-oriented methodologies traditionally used for measuring performance and rewarding salespeople, such as unit volume, gross margin per sales, and gross margin per product. Instead, suppliers are adopting new measures that offer a more appropriate and complete indication of individual contributions to enduring return from customer relationships.

These new indicators include both short-term financial transactions and longer-term relationship enhancement measures such as order accuracy, fill rate, response time, customer satisfaction, cycle time, and defect rate. They form the basis for reconsidering the performance measurement and compensation approach for employees in all customer-coverage positions—the entire customer-coverage team. However, measuring long-term relationship activities and short-term financial results presents a dilemma which many firms are currently struggling to redefine.

MEASURING RESULTS VERSUS ACTIVITIES

Many reengineering efforts call for complete revisions in how the firm interacts with customers, internal departments, and technology as firm members perform their jobs. So, if people need to work differently, then shouldn't the company pay them for working the right way? While this idea sounds great, it has some serious drawbacks. For example, a financial services company was committed to the concept of rewarding activities. The company developed ten new measures that tracked customer satisfaction, leadership effectiveness, and adherence to new selling philosophy, and viewed these measures as necessary complements to the traditional five measures of sales volume and product mix. As the company discovered later, incorporating all 15 performance measures into compensation and recognition programs was overly complicated, and the firm ran the risk of confusing and misdirecting the employees. When it tried to narrow down the list of performance measures, it faced a dilemma that many other companies face: Should the firm pay for financial results or the nonfinancial results that might lead to strong financial performance?

We are all too aware of the mixed track records of companies that have won quality awards but have failed to produce attractive financial results. It now seems clear that a single-minded pursuit of quality may or may not yield financial success. The solution to the dilemma is to measure, but not pay for, all of the nonfinancial results that build enduring returns with customers.

Another method some companies use to reward execution of nonfinancial aspects of the new approaches to customer engagement is to torque their performance-measurement systems. These companies put teeth in their performance reviews by adopting probation systems. Essentially, they make adherence to the new approach a condition of continued employment. If employees do not demonstrate that they can perform well on the nonfinancial measures, they receive a "below expectations" rating. The second occurrence of such a rating results in a probation warning, and the third results in termination. Such an approach gives managers the responsibility for ensuring implementation of the new approach, rather than relying on the pay plan to do the managing.

PAYING FOR CUSTOMER SATISFACTION

Many companies are investigating or talking about paying for customer satisfaction, but few companies are doing it. We surveyed numerous companies and found that few firms are actually paying their salespeople for customer satisfaction, even though 35 to 45 percent of them considered trying to win the Baldrige Award for Quality. There are a number of reasons for this low number. First, many companies are still refining their customer satisfaction measurement techniques. Second, they have not yet defined how to apply those measurements to the ongoing performance of individual personnel or teams.

The solution to the first problem is often quite simple: Begin measuring and then revise the measurement system as its weaknesses become apparent. There are issues that surround the task of designing a survey instrument, but some companies get lost in debating how they will use the information before they even have it. It is not necessary to define a use for the information before it's in hand. The solution is to simply take the first step and start measuring customer satisfaction. As companies build their databases of information and begin to see what the data is saying, they can then make informed decisions on how to use the data and refine the survey methodology.

One often-debated survey design issue is whether to use a single question to summarize the customer's overall satisfaction; for example, "On a scale from 1 to 7, rate your overall satisfaction with our company." Another approach is to create a composite score of the customer's satisfaction based on a mathematical summary of the customer's responses; for example, satisfaction ratings for sales and service are weighted more heavily than satisfaction ratings on logistics or finance. Again, there is a simple answer: Use both approaches and once you have the data, decide which one works best through statistical analysis; for example, determine whether the overall or composite score has a higher correlation with customer retention.

The second problem—measuring customer satisfaction at the level of the customer team—is more difficult. Any company that has a new customer satisfaction measure has a lot to learn before using it in a compensation plan. While it is possible to generate great correlation statistics between customer satisfaction and financial results on a national level, obtaining rational and predictable "behavior" from the same measure at the salesperson or territory level is a totally different matter. For example, what does it mean if a team has good revenue results and low customer satisfaction? What if the customer purchasing agent didn't get along with the loading dock supervisor, but thought highly of the salesperson?

In addressing the question of how to summarize the customer's satisfaction, we have found that a single-question approach has some significant advantages:

- The field will grasp it more quickly because it is simpler.
- There is less for the field to dispute. The single question is final and conclusive in its own right. The composite score, however, is based on dimensions of customer satisfaction, any

one of which can be argued to have greater or lesser relevance in certain customer situations or parts of the country, for example.

- The single question is easier to study from a statistical perspective because there are fewer "moving parts" to understand.

The composite score, however, has some unique advantages. First, it can be built with behaviorally anchored rating scales (BARs), which give clear and direct feedback to customer-coverage personnel. Another advantage is that high or low customer ratings can be explained, because ratings on each dimension can easily be reviewed.

Once a company has customer satisfaction data, it can start to study these issues and develop answers. This is the process of learning to use customer satisfaction information, and the process takes time. To base rewards on a new measure before learning how it operates, however, is asking for trouble.

INTRODUCING NEW MEASURES

Often a reengineered organization needs to assess performance based on a new set of measures. Our benchmarking studies on successfully implemented compensation plans found that the leading cause of failure is the too-rapid adoption of a new performance measure. Adopting a new performance measure is a serious matter. It is the most difficult compensation change a company can undertake. Introducing a new performance measure is like teaching a new language. Employees have to learn a new set of practices, techniques, and working habits, and adjust a perspective built over a working lifetime. And they have to learn what they have to do to make the new number go up or down. If they don't learn the language of the new performance measure, the new compensation plan becomes the "transplant that the body rejects."

One large insurance company introduced a profit orientation

to its sales force by shifting from units to dollars. After a year on the new program, the company deemed it a failure. They were shocked at the number of unanticipated problems in switching to dollars. Their dollar target was way under what it should have been, given the planned rate increases of the firm, which created an unearned windfall for salespeople. Furthermore, their salespeople had not been trained to think in dollars, but were accustomed to constantly converting units to dollars. As a result, salespeople never really understood how the new plan worked or what they were earning. The conversion from units to dollars when reading sales reports or verifying monthly paychecks depended on rates that varie d significantly by product and group. There was no discernible pattern linking the unit plan to the dollar plan. The result was an overly complex pay plan which described how the firm made money but not how its sales staff could make money.

Another information services company developed a new concept for measuring customer and territory profitability, and many support programs were put in place to help sell more profitably. However, the new profit-performance measure was never put in place. The new customer concept was great, but the company's accounting and information systems were ultimately incapable of generating the new performance numbers.

The best way to guard against the risks of a new performance measure is to test the new performance measures without connecting them to pay for at least six months. Report the new measure, but continue to base pay on the old measure. This way, errors in information systems can be detected and corrected, and the work force can learn the new language of the new performance measure. Testing a new performance measure also offers a side bonus: behavior will start to change before pay is shifted to the new measure. We have seen this phenomenon again and again—measuring what you want is almost as effective as paying for what you want. The test puts the proverbial writing on the wall, giving the firm time to prepare to use the new performance measure.

As increasingly useful information systems allow suppliers to measure performance, effectiveness, and costs, they will also allow the supplier to push information down to its front-line personnel. These information systems will also be able to mirror the decision processes the supplier wants followed so that customer-coverage personnel will have the ability to make the judgments they need to make. As that process continues over the next decade, more customer-coverage personnel will be able to grapple with the ultimate measures of firm success: customer goodwill, customer-based profitability, and decisions that improve enduring return from customers.

A major task for suppliers will be aligning their hard wiring—their information systems—and their soft wiring—their reward systems and recruitment and training programs—to support the new behaviors needed to sustain competitiveness.

DEVELOPING EARLY WARNING SYSTEMS

How does a firm know when it must change in a hurry or has the time to make incremental progress? We believe it is rarely appropriate to undertake a quantum-shift change of the processes and personnel that interface with customers. Such a dramatic shift is only appropriate when the firm's customer base, operational foundation, or financial health is in jeopardy. A prerequisite for sensing as early as possible when this might be occurring in time to avoid the disruption of a quantum-shift change is to develop a system for assessing external indicators about customers and competitors and internal indicators about key performance and profitability measures.

This chapter provides a tool—the early warning system—for highlighting when it is time to reposition the total product offering, improve execution, or reduce costs.

BUILDING AN EARLY WARNING SYSTEM

An early warning system seeks to inform management on a timely enough basis about the firm's competitive strength and organizational effectiveness as reflected by the firm's performance relative to earlier performance levels in three major asset categories.

1. Customer base stability

2. Its operational proficiency

3. Its human capital efficiency

Suppliers can put together an early warning system around indicators like the ones captured in the dials sketched in Figure 9-1. Taken in summary, these indicators will scan the relative strength of the firm in each of the three critical asset categories. While the particular early warning system shown in Figure 9-1 can be used to track more than 25 different external and internal indicators, ranging from market size to sales volume, each firm should build an early warning system around the indicators which best pertain to that firm and its industry.

CUSTOMER-BASE STABILITY INDICATORS

CUSTOMER-BASE STABILITY. (See Figure 9-1.) As we have seen, customers tend to stay longer with a smaller number of suppliers than ever before. Four indicators can help a supplier assess the directional trends of the customer base.

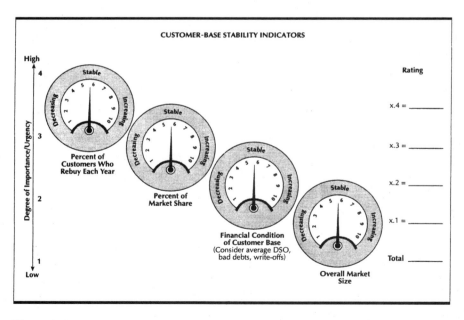

Figure 9-1

- Percent of customers who rebuy each year
- Percent of market share the firm has enjoyed over past three years
- Financial condition of customer base (consider average DSO and bad debts and write-offs)
- Overall market size for the products and services offered by the firm

CUSTOMER PROCUREMENT CAPABILITIES INDICATORS. (See Figure 9-2.) These four indicators can help a firm measure the speed at which customers appear to be strengthening their procurement capabilities.

- Speed with which the number of suppliers the customer base

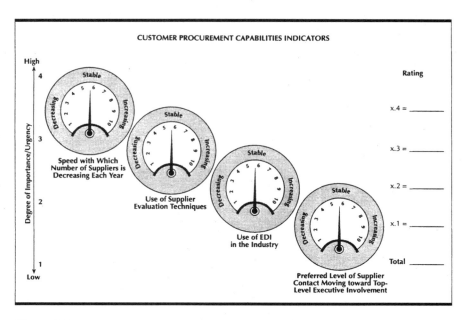

Figure 9-2

is using is decreasing each year (source from annual procurement surveys)

- Customer use of supplier evaluation techniques
- Use of EDI
- Preferred level of supplier contact, ranging from purchasing agent to top-level executive involvement

CUSTOMER BUYING TREND INDICATORS. (See Figure 9-3.) These four measures can be used by a firm which uses a two-tier distribution channel to serve its customers.

- Net new customers last year
- Percent of sales volume from the 20 percent of customers who are the largest purchasers
- Sales through average distributor

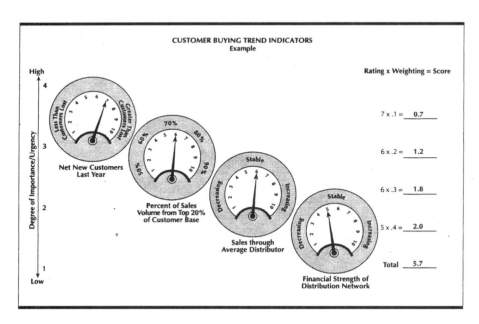

Figure 9-3

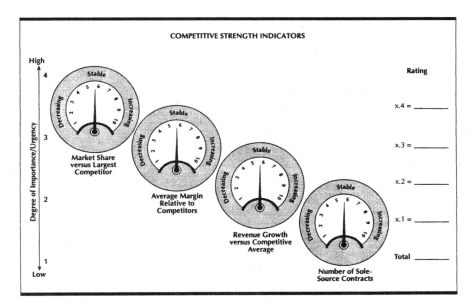

Figure 9-4

• Financial strength of distribution network in the current year

COMPETITIVE STRENGTH INDICATORS. (See Figure 9-4.) These four indicators require gathering more precise information about the competitors than the informal "heard-on-the-street" gossip which often passes for competitive data.

• Market share versus largest competitor
• Average margin relative to competitors
• Revenue growth versus competitive average
• Number of sole-source contracts

INDICATORS OF OPERATIONAL PROFICIENCY

If the investments required to establish and sustain a competitively differentiated position throughout the engagement process

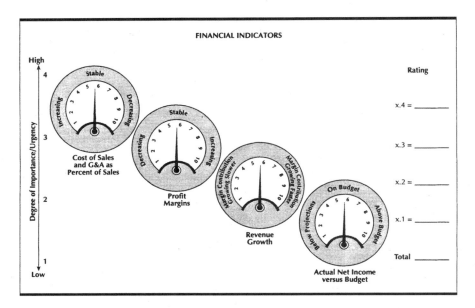

Figure 9-5

are not recaptured in improved profit contribution levels, it will be demonstrated as these measures show a decline over time.

FINANCIAL INDICATORS.   (See Figure 9-5.)

- Cost of sales and G&A as a percent of sales
- Profit margins
- Revenue growth
- Actual net income versus budget over past two years

OPERATIONAL QUALITY INDICATORS.   (See Figure 9-6.) The firm's capability to execute its strategy can be assessed by examining whether these indicators are showing improvements or erosion.

- Customer satisfaction levels

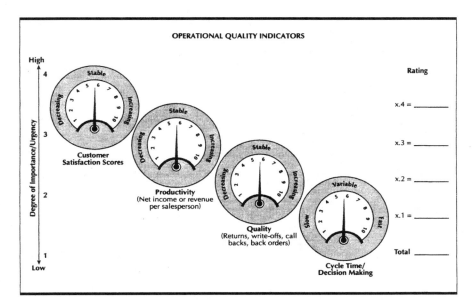

Figure 9-6

- Productivity—net income or revenue per salesperson
- Quality—returns, write-offs, callbacks, back orders
- Cycle time/decision making

HUMAN CAPITAL EFFICIENCY INDICATORS. (See Figure 9-7.) Firms can select from several indicators of firm efficiency at recruiting and organizing their human resources.

- Number of management levels in the organization
- Spans of control
- Customer-coverage employee labor costs as a percentage of sales
- Sales force turnover rate

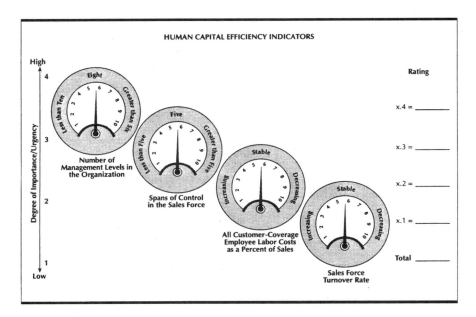

Figure 9-7

DEVELOPING AN EARLY WARNING SYSTEM

For a particular firm to develop and use an early warning system, executives and managers should work collaboratively to complete the following steps:

1. *Appoint a team to select those indicators which best analyze potential problems.*
2. *Through discussion, refine the initial framework by reducing the list of possible indicators to the four most relevant key indicators for each asset category.* For example, the company in the example in Figure 9-1 chose four particular indicators to assess the solidity of the customer base.
3. *Using input from team members, calibrate overall performance for each indicator.* First, answer for each dial (see Figures

9-1 through 9-7) as to the firm's situation and performance measure two years ago. Then, for each dial, assess last year's situation and performance. Finally, answer for the current year. In what direction is the three-year trend for the firm's overall assessment score? In what direction is the trend in each category? What observations and conclusions about the trends in each category can be assembled? What will happen if the trends continue?

For example, in Figure 9-3, net new customers was greater than customers lost, meriting a rating of 7 on the dial. The percentage of sales volume from the top 20 percent of the customers was 65 percent, so that rating is 6. Average sales through distributors were increasing somewhat, producing a rating of 6. Finally, revenue growth versus competitors was decreasing somewhat, producing a rating of 6. Overall, the rating of 5.7 reveals significant customer-base stability at the firm analyzed in this example.

4. *Weigh the relative significance of each indicator based on its ability to measure performance in each asset category.* In the examples, each indicator is given a degree of importance or urgency from 1 to 4. This degree, multiplied by the rating on the dial, provides an overall rating for each indicator. Added together, the indicator ratings yield an overall rating for the asset category.

5. *Compile the ratings for each asset category into an overall score for each of the last three years and then evaluate the organization's performance in light of the score.* If the supplier uses four indicators for each of the three categories, a total score of 35 to 50 indicates that the supplier is in a strong competitive position. A score of 20 to 34 indicates that some change is needed to gain over competitors. A score of 5 to 19 indicates that a massive change effort may be necessary.

An example of a final summary is shown in Figure 9-8. The overall score for the year is 20.5. This supplier certainly must make

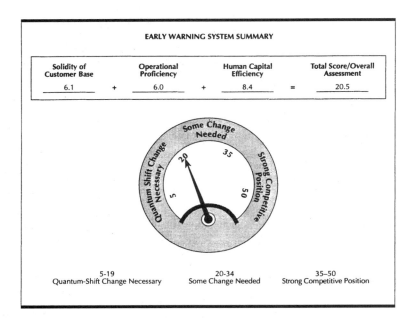

EARLY WARNING SYSTEM SUMMARY

Solidity of Customer Base		Operational Proficiency		Human Capital Efficiency		Total Score/Overall Assessment
6.1	+	6.0	+	8.4	=	20.5

5-19
Quantum-Shift Change Necessary

20-34
Some Change Needed

35–50
Strong Competitive Position

Figure 9-8

some changes toward improving its level of engagement return. The supplier may be able to do this by either repositioning or improving the level of execution, or redirecting costs to deliver the desired level of competitive position through reengineering. Other suppliers with higher ratings still need to reflect on the scores. If the trend is positive, is it positive enough? If the indicators show stable performance, is top management comfortable with the trend, or should the organization be reaching for more? If trends are rapidly declining, what can be done to turn things around?

USING THE DIALS

The customer-base indicators allow a supplier to track either its largest and most important customers or all of its customers well enough to anticipate that changes in the procurement perspectives of that group of customers require the change efforts necessary to maintain enduring customer loyalty.

The indicators for assessing customer procurement capabilities can be applied to individual customers, to customers who fall within the first 20 percent of the 80/20 rule, or to all customers. The gaps which show up between these various choices can tell a supplier which customers it should start with when it reengineers. If the supplier begins by taking the 80/20 rule and then goes through the customer base in 20 percent increments of profitability before deciding which segment of customers to position and execute around, the supplier may be able to narrow the investment, the time, and the money reengineering requires. Reengineering for depth, not breadth, means reengineering around those customers where the enduring return is likely to be higher.

Having the executive team answer these questions and debate these issues will help the firm plan and act early enough to give the organization the time to make changes before being handicapped by poor financial results. The early warning system provides an overall assessment of when significant strategic or reengineering efforts are required. Once the performance indicators and relative weightings of an early warning system have been developed, it is helpful to analyze the trends every six months and keep score over several years. Trends over time provide a good indication of the supplier's overall health, as well as the effectiveness of actions taken to reverse any downward trends.

THE REENGINEERING PROCESS

This chapter examines how to design a second-generation reengineering effort. We have built these guidelines based on our observations of successful and unsuccessful reengineering efforts over the last several years. Most companies who started first-generation reengineering efforts have used large design teams and have experienced frustration with them. We have experimented with several alternatives to the large design team, and the results are described in this chapter.

A company's thinking about its reengineering process should be guided by the degree of change anticipated or required. Second-generation reengineering is not a movement but a tool to be designed to fit a company's situation. We start this chapter with a discussion of the broad options that a company must choose from before it designs its reengineering process.

DEGREE-OF-CHANGE OPTIONS

When should the supplier choose to undergo a massive reengineering campaign in the hopes that it will lead to a quantum-shift change rather than reengineering for continuous improvement? A company might be well advised to engage in a quantum-leap effort if it is one of the suppliers forming enduring customer relationships in an industry which is shrinking its supply base. Conversely, if a company has a major share of stable relationships with the industry's largest customers, then it may be more advisable to pursue reengineering efforts which focus on continuous improvement.

Figure 10-1 supplies the rationale for selecting the right change approach within the context of the firm's needs. We see three major options for a reengineering effort. First, a company can pursue the quantum-leap approach proposed in the early literature surrounding reengineering (for example, Hammer and Champy, *Reengineering the Corporation*, 1993). However, we have seen too many reengineering efforts choke on the philoso-

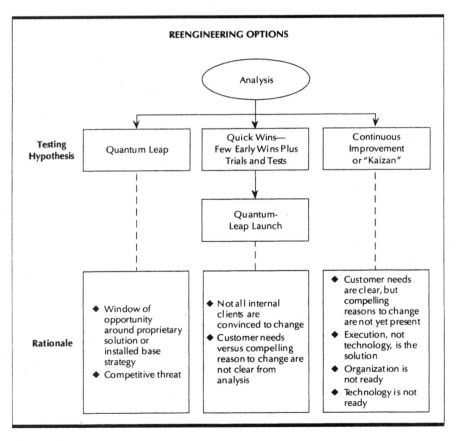

Figure 10-1

phy of massive change. This has led us to conclude that, while many companies need to reengineer their processes, most cannot do so radically.

Two other reengineering options are available. First, companies can look for narrow improvement opportunities during the early phases of reengineering (the "quick-win" approach). These enhancements are made as a broader, more radical vision of the change effort is being completed and tested. Reengineering purists would scoff at diverting the company's attention away from designing and implementing the quantum shift. But, the company needs a higher success rate, and the quick-win approach is one way to increase the positive impact of reengineering.

Second, companies can accept the challenge of crafting a radical vision for their future, but then develop intermediate designs that move the company forward in a pattern of continuous improvement toward the bold future vision. As employees make changes and see success, the vision becomes more believable and attainable.

The quantum-shift approach of first-generation reengineering is most appropriate when there is a limited window of opportunity. The best opportunities for radical reengineering occur when there is already a break or a change in production, such as a major new product line rollout, or some other dramatic event that might cause a natural and radical shift in the business—a merger or an immediate and substantial competitive threat, for example.

The quick-win approach is attractive when a company recognizes it has some major flaws in its approach to customers. These can be addressed with a reengineering effort that first establishes a broad vision for the future, then immediately plunges into the detail of making a limited number of immediate corrections that can have quick payoffs. It is practically impossible for a company to address practical improvement opportunities if management initially stresses radical, quantum-shift change; the design team will be too concerned with radical change to address incremental improvement.

The continuous improvement approach to reengineering begins with a radical vision for the future and assumes that many pieces of the company's operation must be enhanced incrementally and simultaneously. More realistic expectations are set for the pace of change, and enhancements are developed and implemented over the course of years. In observing first-generation efforts, we have concluded that a gradual rollout of enhancements is indeed a more accurate description of the actual pace of change anyway. There are two very real impediments to rapid change, especially of customer contact areas of the company. First, employees do not change their behaviors and expectations that quickly. Second, customers change even more slowly.

Firms can use the early warning system described in Chapter 9 to determine whether recent trends indeed indicate that they are slipping fast enough to warrant a quantum-shift change effort, or whether they have the time to proceed more deliberately.

Personnel readiness is a major factor in setting the speed of a second-generation reengineering effort. If numerous firmwide organizational change efforts in the past have already proven the viability of radical change within the firm's culture, then the company may be ready for a quantum leap. Another factor is the length of time it takes to effectively overhaul an organization's information systems. A quantum leap may not be possible if reconfiguring the firm's information systems lags too far behind the company's other requirements.

DESIGN TEAM OPTIONS

In addition to exploring the pace of the change options, we also urge companies to consider alternative design team structures. The design team approach to securing participation is the second critical issue for reengineering. Participation has a major impact on design quality, the start-to-finish cycle time of the reengineering process, employee buy-in, and implementation effectiveness.

LARGE DESIGN TEAM

First-generation reengineering secures the employee consensus necessary for change by encouraging participation through a large design team. Large design teams may include 30 or more people. The teams reach these sizes to achieve cross-functional, geographic, and hierarchical representation. Large design teams can be effective, but they tend to be very slow to complete their work. And, more importantly, they can become uncontrollable by assuming unexpected power and influence in the company. Executives who are experienced in previous change efforts can easily solve the problem with large design teams: The entire firm can be internally focused until the design team finishes its work.

No design team will always develop a 100 percent perfect design. But the large design team spends so much time on developing its design, and develops so much internal commitment to the design, that it is exceedingly difficult to give this large group negative feedback. When senior management rejects or asks for modification of part of the design, ill will with design team members can develop, possibly creating a major embarrassment for management. Other times, if management disagrees or finds that the cost of implementing the proposals is excessive, management may resort to delay tactics or diversions to avoid an outright rejection of the design team's recommendations. If this happens, employees can become disillusioned and morale may decline.

Second-generation reengineering offers two other design team participation options that are more effective: the corporate design team and the two-tiered design team.

CORPORATE DESIGN TEAM

An alternative to the large design team is the corporate design team. This group is smaller, with 7 to 15 members. It is staffed largely by a cross-functional collection of corporate staff executives. A few representatives are also included from lower levels in the organization. This corporate group is much more efficient and does not develop a metaphorical life of its own, since it is a subset of the company's leadership.

CROSS-FUNCTIONAL REPRESENTATION.   A key difference from first-generation efforts is that the corporate design team should include representatives from the sales organization. The corporate design team should also include representatives from customer service, marketing, and distribution (including warehouse and delivery), plus any other functions that have regular customer contact. In some industries, for example, there may be major issues arising from accounts receivable, and personnel from this function should be included on the design team. In some cases, the finance department may play a customer-coverage role. The greater the amount of direct contact with customers that the employees in a particular function have, the greater the need for that function to be represented on the corporate design team.

MULTILEVEL REPRESENTATION.   Part of the need to ensure cross-functional representation while limiting team size can be met by placing executives with broad functional responsibilities on the corporate design team. Some multilevel participation is also useful to avoid the "groupthink" that sometimes results when all team members are drawn from the same level in the organizational hierarchy. On the whole, however, second-generation reengineering is less concerned with the issue of levels than first-generation forms, which mandate direct grass-roots participation. Second-generation corporate design teams may be made up entirely of second- and third-level managers who solicit grass-roots input through interviews and focus groups.

TEAM SIZE.   The need for cross-functional and multilevel representation and the equally important value of a small team function together like three factors in a single equation. The corporate design team should be limited in size to 15 members or fewer—7 may be optimal in many cases. Within this size constraint, the firm must deal with the need for cross-functional and multilevel representation.

Generally, the larger the design team, the more time it will take for the group to learn to work smoothly and the more hierarchical the group will be. When large teams meet, there are usually primary, secondary, and tertiary contributors, which often results in team members developing only partial commitments to the design being generated. Large teams are also more likely to foster stonewalling and sandbagging.

FINANCE PERSONNEL. In first-generation reengineering, finance people were sometimes called on to provide support for the design team but were rarely appointed to serve as team members. In second-generation efforts, it is becoming more important for finance people to sit on the team. These are usually individuals who have clear knowledge about the contribution that the sales, marketing, and service functions make to the organization—their real impact on costs and profitability from customers. They may be senior financial analysts, assistant vice presidents for finance, or special projects personnel. The key is that they know how the firm makes money, not just how the firm *counts* money.

CONSULTANTS. Many companies that are pursuing second-generation reengineering are using some form of third-party expertise. This is often helpful. One common problem with design teams is that members are still expected to meet their other job responsibilities. The team may be forced to cut corners. When it does, one of the first tasks to go is analysis. Analysis is important because it helps ensure that accurate conclusions are reached regarding potential benefits and costs. This is one reason that it is helpful to hire outside consultants—they ensure that appropriate analyses are completed.

Another task that is often set aside is the writing—the codification of the team's proposals and the reasoning behind their recommendations. It is wise to put a strong writer on the design team or to use consultants for this purpose. Consultants can provide critical support in documenting the team's work.

Consultants can also help open up the process and present issues from a totally different perspective—that of the experienced observer of the best practices and retroactive regrets of other firms who have tried the same kind of solution. Sometimes it is easier for the consultant to play the role of obnoxious outsider, asking tough questions and introducing a healthy level of irreverence for the past.

SUPPORT PERSONNEL. The design team can also call on support personnel to gather information, make meeting arrangements, prepare analyses, conduct interviews, or provide clerical assistance. Using support personnel is another way to maximize cross-functionality while limiting the size of the team—by having support personnel serve, but not "vote" on the team. If the firm wants to include manufacturing on the design team, for example, it can do this directly by appointing manufacturing personnel or indirectly by assigning the personnel to act as a support to the team.

CORPORATE DESIGN TEAM EXAMPLE. A legal publishing firm formed a corporate design team that included the following positions:

- Marketing and sales vice president.
- Sales vice president.
- Product manager from business unit A.
- Product manager from business unit B. (These product managers did not represent all or most of the company's products, but they covered some of its biggest products.)
- Finance. (This was not the head of finance, but someone who knew all the numbers and had a great interface capability with systems.)

- Customer service manager.
- Telemarketing manager.
- Direct-mail manager.

Because of the nature of its business, the company decided that its team should represent different functions and different channels: sales, telemarketing, and direct mail. For this firm, these were the key customer-touching positions.

No corporate design team is complete without a plan for obtaining input from a broad cross section of employees at grass-roots levels. There are two techniques for achieving this objective: *full-participation meetings* and the *two-tiered design team.* Each will be described subsequently.

Full-Participation Group Meetings

The best technique we have seen for achieving broad input is the full-participation group meeting. These meetings have up to 50 people in attendance and last between four and six hours. The people meet as a large group and also as members of small groups. A full-participation meeting might follow this agenda:

1. A presentation is made to the whole group. Background on a particular issue and the overall process being followed by the corporate design team is provided.

2. A set of tasks to be accomplished by small group breakout meetings is described. For example, the small groups could be asked to select a group recorder, craft a vision of a customer's ideal experience with the company, and select a group presenter.

3. The large group breaks out into smaller groups to complete the task. These small groups have 10 or fewer employees with as much diversity as possible—cross-functional, multilevel, and mixed gender, race, and age—"max-mixes" of employee characteristics.

4. At the end of the allotted time, the large group reconvenes and a reporter from each of the small groups presents the small groups' findings to the larger group. The original group of 50, for example, hears 5 presentations from the 5 smaller groups.

5. Clarifying questions from the large group are fielded by the small group presenters or other small group members.

6. The large group is asked to make concluding or integrating comments and observations. Comments are collected and categorized in order to find similarities and differences among the different presentations. After this session, the large group can move on to another task or split into small groups again to develop a refined vision based on input from the large group.

7. Presentations are recorded and distributed. The presentations are keyed into a computer, printed out, and distributed. These proceedings are reviewed and modified by the large group and produced in a final document. All participants (and all employees as well) receive copies of the proceedings.

Corporate design teams have found that they can obtain rich input from such meetings. And, by holding several, it is possible to quickly build up a large sample size. The large sample size, in combination with broad distribution of the proceedings, can build a very effective sense of employee participation in the reengineering effort.

TWO-TIERED DESIGN TEAMS

The other technique for obtaining input from a broad cross section of employees at grass-roots levels is the two-tiered design team approach. The two-tier option takes a phased-in, two-step approach to participation. In the first phase of the process, the corporate design team sets the broad principles and vision for reengineering. The corporate design team may solicit employee input or test its ideas in focus groups, but participation is not a key objective being pursued. In the second phase, a local design team is chartered. This is where grass-roots employee involvement is obtained.

The transition between the corporate and the local design team has two components: a set of *principles* that must be adhered to and a set of *suggestions* for consideration. The suggestions can be provided in the form of straw models—draft details on compensation, job design, and sales cycles, for example—that the local design team can respond to, modify, or approve. Two examples of the two-tiered approach are summarized as follows:

1. A firm in the legal publishing industry placed managers from sales, marketing, and customer service on the corporate design team. This group conducted interviews and focus groups with employees and customers and conducted extensive data analyses. With a consultant, they then put together a radical vision of how to improve service to customers through a redesigned sales and service cycle.

   The local design team included two individuals from the corporate design team. Sales, service, and telemarketing people made up the rest of the local design team. Broad design parameters and strategy were established as givens. Then the local design team focused on job design, performance measures, and implementation.

2. A company in the automotive industry gathered HR representatives from all its different business units to participate on the corporate design team. They outlined the basic principles for a new approach to rewards. One of the broad principles generated by the corporate design team was to increase dramatically the use of variable pay. Local design teams were formed to develop the detailed application of variable pay to various employee groups. The local teams were charged with detailed design and implementation responsibility.

Selecting the Right Process Option

Companies can select between the full-participation and two-tiered approaches by reviewing the criteria summarized in Figure 10-2. Each of these criteria is discussed in detail as follows:

1. *Degree of change needed.* A company that wants to pursue a radical design is probably wise to select the full-participation option. The challenges and solutions that arise from full participation are usually more wide-ranging and dramatic than the ideas that arise in a more controlled and hierarchical two-tiered approach.

2. *Amount of buy-in required.* If the changes that will be created by reengineering are significant and potentially unsettling, the employee buy-in that occurs with full participation will help ease the transition and promote successful implementation. Also, at companies where individual contributions are critical, the full-participation approach may be the appropriate course. The greater the amount of participation, the less likely that the employees involved will discount the new design.

3. *Control and risk.* As participation increases, control decreases.

Criteria	Full-Participation	Two-Tier
SELECTING THE RIGHT REENGINEERING DESIGN PROCESS		
Degree of Change	✓	
Amount of Buy-In	✓	
Control and Risk		✓
Education	✓	
Research		✓
Company in Trouble		✓
Downsizing		✓
Midcourse Flexibility		✓
Continuous Improvement	✓	
Time Frame	✓	

Figure 10-2

The full-participation approach is less controllable than the two-tiered approach. If the company provides a direct and explicit way for the great majority of employees to express their ideas, and these employees indicate that they overwhelmingly support a particular course of action, it is very difficult for top management and the design team to set off on an utterly different direction. However, even though the full-participation option entails a higher risk, it also provides a much higher return, because there is extensive employee buy-in, education, and involvement.

4. *Education versus research.* Education is stressed in the full-participation option, in which a large part of the objective is to educate the participants along the way. The two-tiered design option is more concerned with getting the right information and the right answers.

5. *Company in trouble.* A company in dire straits might be more inclined to select the two-tiered design option because it necessitates that the company pull inward, maintain tight control, and move quickly. Also, the two-tiered design option is especially well suited for identifying and implementing quick wins, which is particularly relevant for a company in trouble. But a company that is facing low employee morale or high employee resistance to change might be more inclined to go with the full-participation option because it encourages employee buy-in.

6. *Downsizing.* If it is likely that the company will have to downsize, it is possible to use the full-participation approach, but it may be preferable to take the two-tiered option. Some companies, however, have used the full-participation approach when downsizing was part of the reengineering plan. These companies asked the employee groups to develop the criteria for downsizing. In one of these cases, the employee groups developed plans for downsizing through retirement and early retirement, job sharing, and other methods that were accepted by the work force.

7. *Midcourse flexibility.* A company that takes the two-tiered approach and is not satisfied with the amount or type of participation can always add focus groups or local design teams to approximate full participation. But once a company has announced a series of full-participation meetings, it is difficult to back off from that commitment and return to a two-tiered format.

8. *Continuous improvement.* The broad educational aspect of full participation results in a stronger emphasis on continuous improvement. While the design process itself creates an atmosphere of challenging established assumptions and encouraging employees to ask questions, continuous improvement spreads farther with full participation than with a two-tiered approach.

9. *Time frames.* Time frames are more predictable with the full-participation option, since the corporate design team maintains control of the process throughout the reengineering effort. Under the two-tier option, control over timing is shared with or partially surrendered to local design teams.

TEAM LEADERS

After selecting the appropriate design team process, it is important to consider the design team's leadership. The design team can be chaired by someone who is at the same organizational level as other team members or by someone who is one level higher. If the leader is too senior, his or her presence can be intimidating. In our experience, a peer can be a successful chairperson. However, it is often difficult for a peer to manage the group process and introduce substantive issues in team meetings. When a chairperson begins to strongly advocate a particular position, objectivity in making decisions around process and procedure becomes suspect. Consequently, if a peer is going to serve as chairperson, it is preferable to choose a peer whose function is not central to the reengineering process. For example, it may not be wise to select a peer chairperson from sales. That person would have difficulty making substantive contributions surrounding new engagement processes as well as managing the overall reengineering process.

The key criteria for selecting the chairperson are outlined as follows:

1. *Out of the box.* The chairperson must be someone who is already "out of the box," that is, someone who can think creatively and is not wedded to the status quo.

2. *Access to top management.* The chairperson must also be someone who has access to top management in the normal process of conducting the job. Access on both a formal and informal basis is important. The chairperson needs to be able to go to top management for guidance or to stay abreast of major team developments such as launching the focus groups.

3. *Group process skills.* The chairperson must be someone who can manage the group process in team meetings. The most successful teams are led by people who set out the agenda and carefully monitor and balance air time, and then orchestrate a consensus on the next tasks to be accomplished and the responsibilities of individual members. Also, the chairperson must know how to limit discussions of process or agenda issues, which often can take over group discussions.

LOCAL DESIGN TEAMS

The local design team typically includes one or two members of the corporate design team. Assigning two members ensures a more balanced perspective. One of these members usually chairs the local design team. Some of the members of the local design team may report directly to members of the corporate design team. For example, several sales managers may serve on the local design team while the head of sales sits on the corporate design team.

The most important point in selecting members for the local design team is to provide representation for the functions that will be most deeply affected by the implementation of the design. The need for cross-functionality was addressed by the composition of the corporate design team and in the broad parameters they established. With the need for cross-functionality already satisfied, the composition of the local design team can be geared to creating the best team for implementation purposes. One company placed its two best regional managers on the local design team. One of these emerged as the person who would run the test of the local design team's final recommendations.

TESTING

The design process typically includes a period of time when new ideas are tested. Tests should be designed to balance two needs. On one hand, tests should be designed to maximize success. For example, experienced salespeople or sales managers may be selected to participate in the test. Or the test may need to be small enough so that initial training can be provided quickly and effectively, with manual tracking and reporting systems in use until automated procedures are in place.

On the other hand, tests should also be designed so that if the test is a success, there is strong reason to believe that a national rollout will be successful. Consequently, a test should not be based on the best employees or the fastest-growing customers in the country. Tests need to expose likely implementation difficulties and provide realistic projections of costs and benefits.

One way to run an effective test is to have a test region and a control group. This can be accomplished by selecting two parts of the country that are similar. Choose one for the test, and compare results in both markets after the test is complete. One company wanted to test the impact of centralized customer services that were previously provided by salespeople. They chose a test and control region, and did not tell the control region that they were being compared to the test region. After the test period, the results of the two regions were compared, and the company found that customer satisfaction in the test region had dropped to unacceptable levels. The company needed to assess its design to determine what caused the drop in customer satisfaction and develop a new design for a second test. Since the initial test was developed and implemented on a small scale with a control group for comparisons, the company was able to test and revise its design in a short period of time. Had a large test been conducted without a control group, the design problems might not have surfaced and been resolved as quickly.

Tests may need to provide hold-harmless compensation arrangements to guarantee, for example, three months' average income. In the control test example just discussed, the company made no change to its compensation plan during the test. Since the test was designed to enhance sales productivity, compensation was expected to increase. Salespeople in the test were told that, if the test was a success, there might be future changes to their compensation plans. Productivity did increase during the test, which consequently led to an increase in compensation.

Such compensation arrangements are designed to direct attention to implementing the new design and to eliminate disruptive concerns about compensation. If there will be a substantial integration of functions and major changes in jobs, it is usually preferable simply to take money out of the picture through the use of guaranteed levels of income for a period of time during the test until the new design is understood and support systems are in place.

During the test phase, the company attempts to determine how much of the new vision represented in the design can be executed. The objective is to assess whether the company needs to back off from the most radical elements of the design to guarantee acceptability or whether it can expect to succeed with the "ideal" design as it stands.

Theoretically, the test also verifies the cost-benefit analysis developed during the design phase. In practice, it is not realistic to completely verify the cost-benefit analysis before determining whether the test is a success. Companies simply can't wait that long. Instead, companies should choose interim indicators of whether the program is delivering the desired results. In the control group example discussed earlier, rather than focusing on the design's return on investment, the company instead focused on customer satisfaction levels in the test and control groups. When they found a drop in customer satisfaction, they knew that design adjustments were required.

Sometime during the process of completing the reengineering process, the company and its employees will enter the "valley of despair," probably in terms of financial results, and perhaps in terms of employee morale and commitment to the vision. Part of the purpose of the test is to determine, before national rollout, how much change the company can bear. The company can then reevaluate the pace of the planned rollout or ensure that its design is viable and practical rather than too radical and unfeasible.

FORMING AND LEADING TEAMS

Today's approach to working with customers is centered around meeting increasingly customized and complex customer needs—needs that frequently cannot be met by individual salespeople. First-generation reengineering selling teams were generally made up exclusively of sales reps organized around a product or geography. Now, companies as diverse as AT&T, Baxter, General Electric, and Sallie Mae have discovered that meeting new procurement requirements and perfecting the overall customer interface requires a customer-focused team (CFT) approach. This approach draws on many of the company's functional experts, from product design to logistics to finance.

A number of organizational benefits can result from the successful use of cross-functional customer-coverage teams. Our clients indicate that their most important objective when they reorganize into teams is *bringing greater knowledge and skill together at one time.* For their organizations, a team whose members bring different skills, backgrounds, and experiences increases the possible combinations of creative and complete solutions to offer when building customer relationships. Learning how to form, lead, and motivate the firm's best sales and nonsales talent to meet the needs of large and demanding customers is an art that senior managers must learn.

TEAMWORK OR TEAM?

Our experiences with clients suggest that it is important to differentiate between when a firm wants *teamwork* and when it wants dedicated *teams*. Cooperative selling efforts and the need for extemporaneous selling teamwork exist in virtually every organization, but may not be recognized as teams, either by label or by the organization through team-based incentives. In order to make this choice, we have found it useful to analyze the firm's approach to customers, management, and employee involvement in how work gets done. Figure 11-1 helps define, from three perspectives (those of customers, management, and employees), whether a firm is a dedicated team or is a traditional organization that desires more teamwork.

Even when the conditions cited in Figure 11-1 describe that

TEAMWORK OR TEAM?

Perspective	Traditional Organization	Teamwork	Dedicated Team
Customer			
◆ Relationship	• Ranges from high-value relationship to transaction or project-driven; historically bound by geography	• Solution driven, tactical with strategic potential • Valued or complex relationship	• Strategic, potential to become partnership • Highly valued and complex relationship
◆ Contact	• One-dimensional through salespeople	• Multidimensional • Employee participation in decisions results in productivity improvement	• Multidimensional • Mutual decision making results in breakthrough performance
◆ Objectives	• Sales revenue goals	• Total revenue/profit contribution/customer satisfaction	• Total revenue/profit contribution/customer satisfaction/long-term success
	• Quantitative goals	• Quantitative and qualitative goals	• Quantitative and qualitative goals
Management			
◆ Style	• Directive, controlling	• Empowered, enabling	• Empowered, enabling
◆ Focus	• Internal, financial	• External and internal Operational and financial	• External, operational
◆ Reporting	• Vertical	• Horizontal/vertical	• Customer/horizontal
◆ Accountability	• Individual/manager	• Team/individual	• Team/individual
Employee			
◆ Commitment	• Committed to own success	• Committed to customer and team success	• Committed to customer and team success
◆ Support	• Requested of multilayered functional silos, not linked to sales	• Requested within function and outside core function	• Requested levels of support within the team
◆ Time Requirements	• Additional responsibility to core job	• Recognition that team membership is significant contribution beyond core job	• Full-time team membership is the job

Figure 11-1

dedicated teams do, in fact, exist in the firm, it is still best to reduce the number of teams to only those whose rationale for existence meets most or all of the criteria cited. Conversely, encouraging greater teamwork when dedicated-team characteristics are clearly desired, but a dedicated team is not yet called for, will yield better results than a sweeping reorganization into teams.

Evaluating whether your organization has the potential for a team-oriented culture does not have to be difficult. Does your firm have a history of employee involvement or decision making in a group setting? Do you use temporary design teams of employees to prioritize problems, resolve issues, and so on? Does the firm have a history of sharing information freely across functional boundaries (for example, companywide job postings)? Does the firm have a history of functions working together to achieve firm goals rather than functional goals? Does the IT system distribute information and communications freely to all functions within the organization?

One final test executives can take before deciding whether they need teamwork or teams is to determine whether they can clearly communicate, and employees will readily agree, that a team-based structure makes the most business sense. This type of commonsense test must be passed if employees and managers are to let go of their traditional work habits and embrace a team approach.

CHARACTERISTICS OF A SUCCESSFUL TEAM

We have found that, regardless of sales strategy and business conditions, successful teams tend to have the following characteristics:

1. Clear definition of the type of teamwork required
2. Adequate support resources where needed (i.e., information systems, leadership, communication)

3. Established performance measures

4. Real decision authority/empowerment of the team

Then, once the team is established, it is important to have a rewards system that supports its objectives. Sometimes teams may be formed on an informal, as-needed basis to satisfy customer needs. In these circumstances, it is difficult to plug individuals into a traditional team-based reward system. Yet it is precisely the integral role these teams play in satisfying customer needs that makes recognition of their contributions to the company's success so critical. When designed properly, such reward systems provide the incentives necessary to reward team members and the entire organization for those performance results that are most valued by the customer.

Focusing on each of the steps outlined in this chapter can help managers who are responsible for building and sustaining successful teams.

ESTABLISH THE ADVANTAGES

The first question executives should sort out before moving their organizations to a team basis for completing work is a strategic one: Will the time and productivity loss required for personnel to be fully effective in a new work style be offset by the results achieved? The results a team might achieve could be considered worthwhile if, when used to work with the most important and profitable customers, they:

- Ensure that the firm's competitive position with individual customer(s) is improved. Often this occurs because the functional approach cannot meld the expertise of each function quickly enough and accurately enough to respond to those customer needs and demands.

- Yield more accurate or cost-effective decisions than a traditional organizational structure.

Working through these questions at the customer-specific level before initiating a team-based culture will ensure that the firm's initial (and, therefore, time-intensive) learnings about team effectiveness will be gained with those customers who present the best opportunities for optimal return on investment.

CLEAR THE OBSTACLES

Knowledge of the clear business advantages that can explain why each team has been formed helps minimize a major obstacle to successful team performance—that is, the senior managers of the affected functional organizations. Senior functional managers can obstruct team effectiveness in three ways: (1) by focusing on individual results, (2) by providing inadequate resource allocation to the team, and (3) by stifling real team authority. Often these obstructions are the result of a genuine inability to reconcile how they can meet their functional responsibilities without a hierarchical sense of control over the resources necessary to meet those objectives.

FOCUSING ON INDIVIDUAL RESULTS. Senior functional managers often retain the means to set individual performance goals. Setting these objectives is often the basis for calculating the rewards payouts to those members of the team whose historical home is that manager's function. For example, the everybody-wins-or-everybody-loses environment to which teams aspire can easily be frustrated by senior managers who continue to reward some team members on the basis of how they meet their individual sales goals. Executives can test whether their teams' members should have team or individual goals by applying the guidelines illustrated in Figure 11-2. This test of the maturity or commitment of the team to achieving results through the team instead of through the accumulation of the individual goal achievements of team members can be used as an important first step in overcoming the objectives of reluctant functional managers.

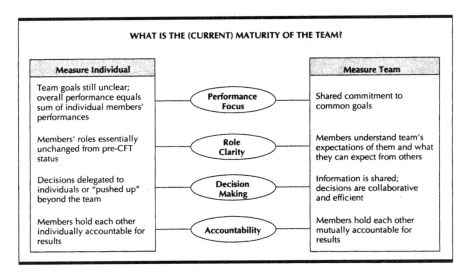

WHAT IS THE (CURRENT) MATURITY OF THE TEAM?

Measure Individual		Measure Team
Team goals still unclear; overall performance equals sum of individual members' performances	Performance Focus	Shared commitment to common goals
Members' roles essentially unchanged from pre-CFT status	Role Clarity	Members understand team's expectations of them and what they can expect from others
Decisions delegated to individuals or "pushed up" beyond the team	Decision Making	Information is shared; decisions are collaborative and efficient
Members hold each other individually accountable for results	Accountability	Members hold each other mutually accountable for results

Figure 11-2

INADEQUATE RESOURCE ALLOCATION.   In many organizations, senior functional managers may also adjudicate whether teams receive the fully committed resources necessary to meet the teams', but not necessarily the functions', goals. This can easily happen when, for example, the senior functional manager of the sales organization keeps the best salespeople to ensure that the sales function meets its goals, and thereby leaves the mediocre salespeople to merge into "teams."

LACK OF REAL AUTHORITY.   Senior managers often want the greater flexibility, coordination, and cooperation of a team-oriented culture but do not want to concede the control or accountability of how work is done to a "team" they can't control. Thus, the firm can have lots of team talk and some team rewards, but it doesn't have teams yet.

CLARIFY ROLES

It comes as no surprise that, just as in other organizational endeavors, selecting the right employees and determining the right mix of skills and the right size of the team is critical to forming a high-performance team. But it is also important to grant and clarify the decision-making process and roles both within the team and elsewhere within the overall organization.

It is easy to conclude intuitively that employees with similar backgrounds, professional skills, and perspectives would be able to get along well and accomplish assigned tasks with a minimum of internal processing time. But those same advantages of similarity may limit their ability to achieve the level of creativity which a cross-functional team decision-making process can optimize. Of equal importance is the preference for members of equal personal and professional power and articulation to be together on those teams that require close and frequent interaction.

For the same reason, each team member should be vital to the team's optimum performance. In some cases, it may be appropriate to designate core or permanent team members and designate others to assist or rotate through the team on an as-needed basis.

While we have worked with clients where the customer-focused teams for one account have approached 90 members, teams larger than 7 or 8 members are generally more difficult to manage and coordinate. One way to build such a large team and take into consideration the greater effectiveness of people working in smaller groups might be to form subteams within the large-team concept.

Executives will find that employees with a lack of team experience will not be long-standing handicaps to team performance if the firm provides some training in conflict resolution, group problem solving, and effective meeting protocols.

If there is one role to which specific attention should be paid, it is that of the team leader. Effective team leaders are a key ingredient in maintaining both internal team relationships and a focus on external performance goals. Individual leadership of a high-participation team can be a source of tension to some organization members who might associate this role with that of a traditional "manager." Typically, these organizations deal with this apparent contradiction in one of two ways:

1. They semantically clarify the role as that of a "coach," not a manager.
2. They focus the leadership role on the team's external relationships with the larger firm around such tasks as:
   a. Dealing with obstacles confronting the progress of the team.
   b. Securing resources required.
   c. Communicating revised goals and objectives as the team changes and reshapes over time.
3. They allow team leadership to be shared or rotated.

While clarity is a specific goal of the managers or "coaches" responsible for leading teams, their focus on clarity can be optimized by helping all members understand why they were selected and what performance goals the team should achieve. Clarifications beyond that point run the risk of being so narrowly defined that they create obstacles to the openness of communication, as well as to the full appreciation of each member's perspective and potential contribution.

SET PERFORMANCE GOALS

Determining performance standards and linking rewards to performance outcomes is crucial to team cohesiveness. To the extent that the firm has historically embraced a combination of top-downwards and bottom-up approaches to setting mutually agreed-upon goals, the team may be expected to work together to set its specific performance targets within the context of broader organization performance expectations. It is through working together to set common initial objectives that team members can become committed to each other and to meeting their team's goal.

In either case, it is not sufficient to just set annual performance goals. Since the team concept suggests a new and amorphous way of working, the need for external quantifiable milestones of progress during the first year of using a team will help reinforce the team's newfound feelings of internal progress.

DEVELOP PERFORMANCE MEASURES. The key to designing incentives that reward team-based selling is to focus on those performance measures that are most valued by the *customer*—industry expertise, inventory management, pricing, or quality, for example—and to *balance* those measures with the strategic business objectives of the *selling organization*—revenue, profit, market share, customer penetration, or strategic product mix, for example. The point is that successful team incentives cannot be designed in a vacuum. They must be carefully planned to consider the company's business objectives and engagement strategies. A company will gain little by measuring for minimal on-hand inventory, for example, if such a measure encourages behavior that undercuts one of its broader business objectives, such as overall on-time delivery to customers. Using Figure 11-3, a company can take the customer analysis a step further and begin to prioritize which customer value-added activities align with important company goals.

As shown in Figure 11-3, several activities clearly could be measures of performance, based on their high rankings with regard to both customer value and the business plan. For example, rapid response to customer inquiries or complaints might be of great importance to some customers, as well as to the success of the business plan. To improve response time, a company may choose to measure improvement over current levels or relative to industry benchmarks. However, if rapid response time is the leading indicator of customer satisfaction and therefore customer retention, improvement in customer retention levels may represent a simpler and more easily calculated measure. Responsiveness may also correlate highly with subsequent sales orders and, therefore, would directly influence customer pene-

DEVELOPING APPROPRIATE MEASURES			
Sales/Service Activities	Value to Customer (1 to 10)	Linkage to Business Plan Goals (1 to 10)	Overall Score*
1. Lead Identification	1	7	4.0
2. Lead Qualification	2	9	5.5
3. Capabilities Demonstration	9	7	8.0
4. Relationship Management	7	9	8.0
5. Product Application	10	8	9.0
6. Product Specifications	9	6	7.5
7. Bill of Materials	6	6	6.0
8. Pricing/Contracts	10	9	9.5
9. Product Delivery/ Installation	10	7	8.5
10. Product Status (availability)	7	9	8.0
11. Product Training	3	5	4.0
12. Credit/Billing	8	8	8.0
13. Product Enhancements/ Updates	3	5	4.0
14. Response to Customer Inquiries/ Complaints	9	7	8.0

Key	
1-3 = Low Value Added	7–10 = High Value Added

* Each score weighted 50%.

Figure 11-3 *Customer analysis by developing appropriate measures of company performance.*

tration. The challenge is to make these distinctions and prioritize those key measures which motivate the achievement of objectives while minimizing redundancy or overpayments for activities which do not lead to results.

In addition to supporting the needs of both the business plan and customers, the selected performance measures must also:

- Be measures for which the firm can develop standards of expected performance that are quantifiable in numerical or other terms—for example, milestones of performance. These standards may be developed from business plan, customer, or industry benchmarks.

- Generate performance results, or meaningful milestones toward performance results, that are attainable within a stated time frame for payout.

- Be measures which can be tracked and reported on a regular basis.

The administrative guidelines of the incentive program must also have provisions which consider factors beyond team members' control, such as suppliers that deliver parts late and hold up orders. In general, measuring a team's performance is quantified by averaging the impact of many experiences. An exception to this rule is a team member who works with a large account and has a single performance objective or even a single sales event for that particular customer.

SELECT MEASURES FOR REWARD PROGRAMS

As we have examined, there is often a whole universe of activities and results that can be measured, but only a few select measures—generally not more than two or three—should be the basis for team member rewards. If the pay plan has more than three measures, participants will deemphasize one or more of the measures in practice by ignoring that measure (or more) and combining others.

When a firm uses multiple measures, they should be weighted to reflect their relative importance in the achievement of overall business and customer results. However, the weight on each single measure should account for at least 10 percent of a team member's total cash compensation. Incentives set below this level generally fail to catch the attention or change the behavior of team members.

A measure that is rewarded in the incentive plan should be one that drives the financial success of the organization. It is critical to ensure that measures intended to drive positive financial results don't, in practice, actually harm the organization. For example, by measuring sales volume, a company may inadvertently encourage indiscriminate selling without accountability for profitability. Although profit contribution is almost always an intrinsically good measure for rewards, other measures, such as margin, may not be. In one sales organization, a sales team was eligible for incentives if the team met certain margin goals. Because payout began only over a specified level of margin, some team members refused to write business that did not meet minimum margin levels, despite having long-term relationships with those customers.

Indicators of progress toward an overall result are generally not included when determining rewards in favor of rewarding actual results. The exception is when, in extreme situations, people in the organization simply will not do certain activities unless they are paid for them. Generally, in these situations, rewards are only temporary (not lasting for more than one year) until the situation is rectified. For example, if a company's accounts receivable cost is escalating because of the increasing number of delinquent accounts, the near-term solution may be to use incentives to reduce the number of delinquent accounts by rewarding better customer qualification and the use of stricter credit terms. Not coincidentally, these are activities the sales team can influence directly. Over the longer term, however, these activities should become a part of the overall job and should not be rewarded directly.

The use of measures that contribute to, or are secondary to, a desired result should be examined carefully. Secondary measures may be used as substitutes for ultimate measures because they screen out extraneous factors. For example, if team members control product pricing but not the fluctuating cost of materials, the measurement of gross margin rather than bottom-line profit may be inappropriate.

Performance measures based on key financial results are appealing candidates for use in reward determination. For example, one insurance company holds field and headquarters teams responsible for loss ratio (sales profitability) because each member plays a different, but integral, role in delivering a lower loss ratio to the company. Field reps can manage loss ratio by better up-front qualification of customers, while headquarters manages loss ratio through better pricing (that is, underwriting) and appropriate expense management.

The bottom line is that any measure directly linked to reward determination should also be linked to achieving the business

WHAT TO MEASURE

Illustrative Sales/Service Accountabilities	Possible Measures	Indicates Progress	Contributory or Secondary Results	Results
1. Pricing/Contracts	• Revenue		3	
	• Margin		3	
	• Profit			3
2. Product Application	• Revenue		3	
	• Market share			3
3. Product Delivery/ Installation	• On-time delivery	3		
	• Customer satisfaction		3	
	• Customer retention			4
4. Capabilities Presentation	• Hit ratio	3		
5. Relationship Management	• Revenue		3	
	• Customer penetration			3
	• Customer satisfaction		3	
	• Customer retention			3
	• Revenue		3	
	• Customer profit			3
6. Credit/Billing	• % Delinquent accounts	3		
	• Average days outstanding		3	
	• A/R cost			3
7. Response to Customer Inquiries/Complaints	• Average response time	3		
	• Customer satisfaction		3	
	• Customer retention			3
		Use to diagnose problems. Only reward in extreme circumstances	Use to assess contributions of key players and screen out extraneous events	Prime territory for performance measurement

Figure 11-4

plan or should have some influence on either customer satisfaction levels or the perceived value of the product. A firm can use the column headings from Figure 11-4 to assess possible performance measures and identify the top candidates for reward purposes.

Conducting the exercise outlined in Figure 11-4 is likely to identify a number of performance measures which might have reward value. However, for the purpose of designing incentive plans, companies must limit these performance measures to the two or three that the sales team can affect most directly and that will produce the most dramatic improvements in the firm's financial results. However, even if a particular measure is not rewarded monetarily but is only used as a performance tracker or financial indicator, it can still serve several important functions for the sales team, by:

- Providing an early indicator that sales performance may be headed off course
- Communicating the critical activities that make up or affect business results
- Testing future performance criteria (for example, reporting customer satisfaction results prior to complete validation of a well-accepted survey methodology)

Besides selecting appropriate performance measures, it is critical to specify the level—company, business unit, region, or territory—at which performance will be measured. Generally, measuring performance at the most available "local" level is preferred or is the most heavily weighted, because it reflects the level at which the team has the greatest influence.

REWARDING TEAMS

Although many firms have discovered that it takes a team to meet a customer's needs, meeting the team's needs sometimes breaks down when the firm tries to put together a team compensation plan, reinforcing the initial skepticism about a team succeeding. The following questions reflect some of the most common roadblocks to designing successful team rewards:

- How do you keep salespeople on a high degree of variable pay, when other team members from nonsales areas have no or low variable pay?
- How do you keep poor performers on high-performing teams from receiving unearned windfall payouts?
- How do you pay according to the role each team member performs for the team?

To answer these questions, we benchmarked seven large sales

forces that have successful team compensation plans. For these purposes, a pay plan was defined as successful when salespeople, sales management, and competitors had a high regard for the team compensation plan, and the plan had been in place for at least three years. Our primary finding from the study was surprising: Successful team compensation plans can be simple and easy to administer.

Some companies achieved this simplicity because they made clean splits with their past individually driven sales compensation plans. One automotive aftermarket company used a 100 percent team plan. They decided that freeloaders were a sales management problem, not a sales compensation issue, and they paid each team member equally, based on the success of the team, not the performance of individual contributors. (This firm dealt with poor performance through the performance management and documentation process until performance improved or individuals were asked to leave the company.) This approach proved to be very effective—the sales force consistently secured the highest market share and the best margins in their category.

Other companies achieved simplicity by defining exactly when to use team selling. A value-added computer reseller used a split-credit formula, without exception, whenever bill-to and ship-to locations fell into different sales territories. Two other companies, one that manufactures power generation, distribution, and control equipment and another that deals in consumer paint products, avoided split credits altogether and, instead, used a double-credit system for sales volume from all national accounts.

Contrast the preceding success stories with the following unsuccessful team plans. A large printing company wanted to provide support to its top salespeople through the use of sales assistants. They offered a cost-sharing solution for the assistant's compensation: the cost of the assistant was shared by the top sales rep and the company. While a few top salespeople used the assistants well and made the plan work, most did not use the program well, preferring to do all the work themselves to save the cost of an assistant; thus, teams were uncommon. This company needed a new mechanism for leveraging salespeople which dealt more effectively with the compensation costs associated with sales support.

To foster a more collaborative selling approach, a large commercial furniture company offered to split credits on a case-by-case basis according to the contribution of each individual on the selling team. Although salespeople tended to specialize by product line, customers bought from all the lines. The company wanted salespeople to help each other close deals in all product lines. However, most salespeople tried to close their deals alone to get all the sales credit and to avoid contentious negotiations with other salespeople.

From these examples of success and failure, it is clear that team compensation does not have to be hard—companies make it hard because they are not fully committed to the concept or they have not figured out exactly when and how it is to be used. The challenge is to move beyond platitudes and discretionary programs. Instead, rules for when to pay for team performance and for handling sales credit must be clear and they must be managed as absolutes. The characteristics of successful team selling plans are outlined as follows:

1. There are clear definitions of who is on the team, what roles are to be played, and how members should work together.

2. There is little or no discretion in determining sales credits—the greater the amount of management interpretation or judgment in allocating sales credit, the lower the effectiveness of the team compensation plan. Measuring individual performance contributions to the team can be done through either a double-crediting system, to encourage teamwork and diminish internal conflicts, or through split-credit systems that reflect distinct and measurable contributions to the sales process. For example, one firm comprising sales and service professionals established a split-credit policy of 70 percent to

the sales and 30 percent to the service rep, respectively, to reflect the level of prominence each had in the sales process.

3. The team performance measure being used has more motivational impact and better reflects "true" performance than individual measures of performance. In other words, although a firm frequently sacrifices individual "line of sight" or degree of impact by using a team performance measure, this weakness can be offset by the greater motivational impact and business relevance of the team measure.

Team-based incentives hold an important place in a total rewards equation alongside base salary, promotions, contests, and recognition programs. To determine just how much of a place they hold (that is, what percentage of pay), it is important to consider external factors like competitive pay mix practices (the amount of fixed versus variable pay typical for the position and the industry), as well as internal considerations, such as the level of direct influence a given team member has on performance results or the firm's ability to set accurate performance targets.

C H A P T E R
T W E L V E

CONTRACTING WITH EMPLOYEES

As we have seen, evolving procurement capabilities are driving second-generation forms of reengineering at a growing number of firms. These realignment and reengineering efforts may require companywide changes that affect virtually every function and every employee. Leading that degree of change and staying in touch with the human component of the strategic equation is one of the greatest challenges executives will face in the coming years. They must be able to fill the conceptual gap between the vision of a profitable corporate future and the rudimentary day-to-day realities of meeting quarterly revenue targets through sales, marketing, and customer-coverage employees learning new ways to work with customers—and, what's more, employees will be worried about their income levels first, and the firm's second.

Many firms claim that they are reengineering to become customer-focused companies. But what does that mean for any one person? How does a sales manager or a marketing manager relearn the way he or she works?

Successful transformation requires executives to prevail simultaneously across a number of fronts. They must win the competitive battle at the point of customer contact despite customers' tendency to constantly "raise the bar" even higher. They must fulfill a larger role in continually finding new ways to create business advantage as the effectiveness of marketing, advertising, and traditional selling strategies diminishes. They must find ways to penetrate ever-changing customer segments with new offerings and new acquisition strategies designed to make an impact despite a proliferation of product and service alternatives.

At the same time, executives must restructure and streamline the firm for both efficiency and effectiveness. In the 1990s, this requires breaking down "silos," competing on speed to market, and minimizing quality deficiencies.

As this chapter discusses, meeting these challenges requires leaders who will, first, understand the performance contract concept; second, spend their own time effectively; third, develop and educate the right people; and, fourth, recognize when they are asking for too much change.

THE PERFORMANCE CONTRACT

Executives are astounded at all of the behavioral and performance management issues that must be addressed in tandem with any process change. These behavioral "glitches" can cause even the best-laid plans to come undone. Too often, the results of the change effort are announced before these issues are resolved or even anticipated.

These understandable concerns and fears will generally come to light when management renegotiates the *performance contract*: the stated or implied understanding between the firm and an individual regarding the individual's role, what the individual is expected to do, and the conditions under which he or she does it. A fully described performance contract also includes standards of performance (what successful performance looks like) and rewards (what an individual will receive for success and what the consequences are for falling short of expectations).

There are three elements to each employee's performance contract that must be renegotiated in order for a change effort to be complete:

1. *Roles:* What the firm is now asking individuals to do and the conditions under which they are expected to operate.

2. *Standards:* What successful performance in their roles would look like.

3. *Rewards:* What individuals will get if they succeed...and the resulting consequences if they fall short.

However, performance contracts, unlike legal contracts, are not negotiated in one or more sessions which come to a conclusion and a binding agreement. They are lived in and recalibrated by employees and managers every working day. Therefore, the tools that managers use to ensure that the basic "blocking and tackling" of the organization is done well must also be redesigned and recommunicated before a change effort can be considered complete. Figure 12-1 outlines some of the clarifications and support tools which must be provided to reanchor the progressive organization.

We believe that the way to develop the clarification and support tools necessary to recontract with each employee is to include first-level managers on the teams that design the new programs. There are several advantages of proceeding in this manner:

1. Participation on the design team serves as a vehicle for further educating the manager.

Performance Contract Elements	Clarifications	Support Tools
Role	◆ Organization structure ◆ Job configurations ◆ Skills and capabilities ◆ Goals	◆ Training and development programs ◆ Performance assessments
Standards	◆ Procedures and protocols	◆ Performance measures ◆ Information flows ◆ Technology needs
Rewards	◆ Performance targets	◆ Incentive plan designs ◆ Recognition programs

Figure 12-1 *Support tools for the change effort.*

2. Involving the *end users* of the support tools ensures full and detailed integration with other management processes, such as merit reviews.

3. By participating, managers are more likely to help create programs that work in the real-life situations of their subordinates. Their sense of the "what-ifs" is grounded in the daily experience of getting people to try new ways of working.

To ensure that each employee understands the new contract, the process for implementing the new clarifications and support tools usually includes multiple one-to-one meetings and communication materials. Firms which pursue recontracting as if they were recruiting and orienting new employees are much more likely to get it right than those firms who merely announce the new organization.

SPENDING TIME APPROPRIATELY

Eras of significant change, such as the era we now find ourselves in, require executives to rethink how they spend their time. To help executives make effective use of their time during and after reengineering efforts, we have constructed what we refer to as the 40/40/20 rule: Of all the time and effort spent leading and managing the customer-coverage organization, spend 40 percent focused externally, 40 percent focused internally, and 20 percent synchronizing the firm's performance management systems. Finally, executives must take the information they gather externally and internally and systematize a continuous cycle of improvement for their firms.

FOCUSING EXTERNALLY

Spending 40 percent of time and effort focused externally means bringing a constant stream of incremental improvements to the firm, as follows:

- Spend 10 percent of time and effort in meaningful discussions with customers about how they are planning to improve and compete for *their* customers. This is perhaps the best and most in-depth way to understand how to help a customer. The effort required to just listen to customers is essential to building on the firm's unique strengths in the marketplace.

- Spend 10 percent of time and effort in building customer relationships. This effort allows the firm to track customer satisfaction and changes in customer procurement strategies.

- Spend 10 percent of time and effort soliciting proposed improvements to customer-coverage capabilities. This assures that these positions remain aligned with customer needs and procurement strategies.

- Spend 10 percent of time and effort "out there" with customers and competitors, attending seminars, benchmarking best practices, and observing technological improvements at other firms. This allows the firm to track the alignment of the competitors' products and services with their customers' needs and procurement strategies.

For example, part of the time spent focusing externally might be spent in meetings with key customers on issues that go beyond the day-to-day details of their long-term relationship with the firm. These meetings would take on a certain complexity. They might investigate how the customer is changing its procurement strategies or procedures or upgrading its purchasing people.

Through these meetings, the supplier could begin to picture the new standards of performance necessary to attract or retain a more loyal or more profitable customer—but also the executional mastery required to lock out the competition. Ultimately, these meetings result in the supplier rethinking the prioritization of resources based on both the customer's anticipated procurement processes and how the customer, in turn, is trying to compete.

Focusing Internally

Focusing internally requires championing the customer and the needs of the customer-coverage personnel to the other internal resources of the firm:

- Spend 10 percent of time and effort shaping the perspective, morale, and quality of other departments' interactions with the customer base and the front-line customer-coverage personnel.
- Spend 10 percent of time and effort improving the competitive effectiveness of all of the firm's messages, scripts, advertising, collateral, direct mail, and telemarketing.
- Spend 10 percent of time and effort developing, analyzing, and communicating the goals and objectives of the firm to the employees.
- Spend 10 percent of time and effort integrating technology, quality improvement, and/or organization reengineering efforts into the cost-effective improvement of the customer-coverage team and the firm's relationship with its customers.

The 40 percent of time spent focusing internally requires sustained attention to better integrating all the subprocesses of the customer management process. This means breaking down functional silos, building cross-functional teams, shaping a horizontal organization, and/or launching continuous education and training programs for all customer-coverage positions. It also means building the customer information systems necessary to track changing customer needs and procurement capabilities and making that information available to all customer-coverage employees.

Synchronizing the Performance Management Systems

The objective here is to bring clarity to the roles and tasks assigned to customer-coverage positions in the field:

- Spend 10 percent of organizational time and effort recalibrating hiring profiles, training methodologies, territory work-load models, the performance management system, and the firm's goal-setting processes.

- Spend 10 percent of time and effort reevaluating the compensation program that ties it all together.

SYSTEMATIZING A CONTINUOUS IMPROVEMENT CYCLE

The way executives can systematize a cycle for continuous improvement is by living the 40/40/20 rule to guide change efforts over both the short and long term. For example, as a part of the 40 percent of time and effort spent focusing externally, try to initiate three competitively distinct enhancements to the firm's product offerings, its delivery system, or the customer's information requests response every 90 days.

Or, as part of the 40 percent of time and effort spent focusing internally, use the following kind of thinking to prioritize a stream of desired improvement:

- Implement three meaningful improvements to administrative support resources, collateral, or training systems every 90 days.

- Implement three communications and information exchange enhancements every six months.

- Conduct thorough account planning reviews every year to analyze new opportunities for competitive distinction through technology, quality improvements, or reengineering efforts.

As part of the 20 percent of time and effort focused on synchronizing the performance management systems, review the effectiveness of the goal-setting processes once a year. Also, review the relevance and clarity of the sales compensation program once a year.

DEVELOP THE RIGHT PEOPLE

Reengineering for enduring and profitable customer relationships means rethinking the skills and knowledge required for customer-coverage positions and managing the existing work force through the reengineering process and the deep organizational change that will surround it. The completion of any change effort often requires modifications in procedures, processes, behaviors, skills, and traits. Traditionally, learning and improving is encouraged in most firms through their performance management systems and training programs.

THE NEW SALESPERSON

One consequence of customer-driven reengineering is that companies will have to field managers and salespeople with skills and knowledge that match those found and used by their customers' cross-functional procurement teams. In a recent survey of procurement officers, as summarized in Figure 12-2, respondents listed the 10 skills and the 10 knowledge areas supplier

Skills and Abilities	Knowledge Areas
1. Interpersonal communication	1. Total quality management
2. Customer focus	2. Cost of poor quality
3. Ability to make decisions	3. Supplier relations
4. Negotiation	4. Analysis of suppliers
5. Analytical skills	5. Lowest total cost
6. Managing change	6. Price/cost analysis
7. Conflict resolution	7. Source development
8. Problem solving	8. Quality assurance
9. Influence and persuasion	9. Supply chain management
10. Computer literacy	10. Competitive market analysis

Source: CAPS, 1993

Figure 12-2 *Desirable traits for suppliers.*

personnel should have that will be most important to procurement employees over the next decade.

Although the surveyed companies offered purchasing training primarily to procurement personnel, 36 percent offer such training to nonpurchasing personnel *and 17 percent offer it to suppliers.* In the future, 58 percent plan to offer purchasing training to nonpurchasing personnel, and 49 *percent plan to offer it to suppliers.*

NEW SKILLS FOR EXISTING PERSONNEL

Existing personnel will need new skills to improve their productivity and to enhance their participation in a wider definition of teamwork. During and after reengineering, the supplier can build a training program around actual problems encountered face-to-face with customers. A good place to begin is by surveying business units for recurring difficulties or tough spots and then taking them into the classroom for solutions. This approach keeps the program and the trainees grounded in the real world of engaging customers. In addition, it often produces new thinking, workable new scripts, and better support materials for overcoming customer concerns or objections.

Second-generation reengineering efforts recast the salesperson in the role of the businessperson who is responsible for making investment decisions to ensure enduring returns from customers and whose compensation is based on the results from those investment decisions. In some cases, companies delegate the decisions of whether to make customer investments to the salesperson—leaving it up to the salesperson or the customer-coverage team to ensure that the capital outlay will result in increased sales—and pay the salesperson or team based, in part, on the ROI from their customers.

Companies may also give a customer-coverage team a budget for the territory, leaving it up to the individual to decide how to divide that budget among T&E, training, secretarial support, advertising and promotion, and other areas to achieve the highest return.

One consumer products company currently provides its salespeople with an open understanding of sales support costs as well as a capped allowance to spend on the resources of their choice. Each salesperson must pay for any additional resources requested. Other companies, like one specialty chemical company, require salespeople to track expenses per customer so that they can develop an account-by-account P&L statement. These plans treat salespeople as businesspeople who are responsible for making decisions outside of the traditional realm of sales—a development that mirrors the expanded roles of their buying counterparts in the procurement function.

THE NEW SALES MANAGER

The more significant the change in behavior that is required in the field, the more important sales or customer-coverage management becomes. Reengineering efforts, no matter how sophisticated, clear, or motivational, cannot overcome significant field management weakness. The stronger field management is, the more sophisticated the change program a field organization can sustain.

SOPHISTICATION AND READINESS. If a company has a fairly high level of sophistication and dedication from its first-level management, it can plan on developing a fairly sophisticated reengineering plan. If not, the executive team may need to focus significantly on management before a substantial change effort is begun. Reengineering success or failure stems from management execution as often as from any strength or weakness in the program itself.

A firm can assess whether it has "sophisticated" managers by reviewing several factors which, once instituted, lead managers to a broader understanding of the business. For example, for how long has the firm provided "business-level" performance reporting to their first-level sales managers? Do first-level sales managers demonstrate a command of the top line of revenue statements and a cost consciousness in their performance reports and goal-setting and budgeting tasks? Does the business expect the business plans developed and submitted by first-level sales managers to demonstrate an understanding of the full range of the company's activities? In addition, does management contain a healthy percentage—20 to 30 percent—of individuals who came from the sales forces of other firms?

Finally, do finance, manufacturing, and marketing work well with first-line sales managers and interact with them frequently? If the supplier's sales managers exhibit all or most of these characteristics, far-reaching reengineering efforts will have a greater chance of success.

POST-REORGANIZATION SALES MANAGEMENT. A number of firms have reengineered for competitive advantage, but their sales executives can't get any traction when the post-reorganization realities cause ambitious plans to slip and slide. Making the reengineering process work commonly falls to the often ill-prepared, largely overlooked first-level managers. If they do not have input into the goals and the choices of the organization, they can't "sell" the new paradigm when it counts on a daily basis.

Sales executives who have participated in Sibson's Sales Force 2000 workshops indicate that, as they reengineer their organizations, they find that they do not need quite so many levels and sales managers as in the past. This is not surprising, given that communications and information-processing advances often circumvent the need for the traditional sales manager role of passing information up and down the organization structure.

However, Sibson's benchmarking studies of major customer-coverage change efforts undertaken at seven *Fortune* 500 firms indicate that sales forces have a temporary increase in their need for communications and training that lasts for at least a year after the new organization is in place. Sales executives might do well to plan for the possibility of fewer sales managers from the start, but to begin reducing the number of sales managers only after reorganization of the field level sales and service jobs is complete.

EDUCATION

In the context of new procurement processes, the reasons customers may rebuy relate directly to their perceptions of the quality of the engagement process: the ease of the exchange, the supplier personnel's business expertise, and the supplier personnel's dedication and sensitivity to the customer's need to compete successfully. As second-generation forms of reengineering create a cross-functional orientation and a customer-focused environment, the success profile for sales representatives and all other customer-coverage employees will become more complex.

The new profile will embrace business management skills, a team/partnership orientation, computer literacy, financial savvy, and a customer-first orientation. As sales jobs continue to change, so will the demands and the need for new training programs. Changes in customer buying practices and new technology will require extensive ongoing training for all customer-coverage positions.

Adding value throughout the engagement process requires skilled personnel with an intimate knowledge of the customer's decision-making process and business objectives. In this sense, training is a central part of the supplier's exchange strategy. Also, the need for cross-functional thinking and service means that managers, support staff, and all customer-facing employees must receive training similar to that of field representatives.

Personnel or the supplier's customer-coverage teams must be able to participate in the buyer's problem-solving process. Product parity often forces suppliers to compete by adding value throughout the customer engagement process. In this new environment, the most important learning results from communications skills: listening to customers, responding to their concerns, and anticipating their needs.

Education must be an ongoing process, not an episodic event limited to new product launches. Customer-coverage personnel must develop their industry expertise well beyond the knowledge required for selling the features of a product line. For example, in the consumer products industry, both salespeople and support people may need to understand both retailer and end-consumer needs. The first goal of any education program is to teach salespeople to listen to the customer's needs and goals and to develop enough of a relationship to form a strategy for ensuring enduring returns with the customers.

BUILDING RELATIONSHIP MANAGERS

As we explored in Chapter 7, the primary strategy for differentiating one firm from all the other firms is to surround the core product offering with industry or application expertise. This can be done only by personnel with a whole new sense of what relationship management skills really will be in the late 1990s and beyond. We believe that within relationship management there are three levels of success. In Figure 12-3, each of those levels is divided in half: one half represents the skill set the personnel

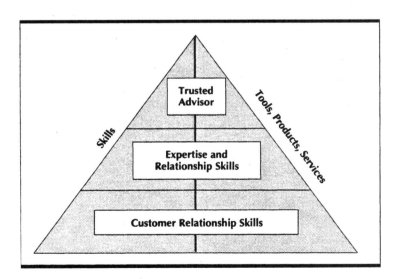

Figure 12-3 *The three levels of success in relationship management.*

must achieve and the other represents the tools, products, and services that the firm must build to support each skill set.

LEVEL ONE: CUSTOMER RELATIONSHIP SKILLS. Figure 12-4 illustrates that the first step and the foundation for relationship management success is developing a clear understanding of the activities and outcomes of the identification and specification processes. That is where the seeds of successful relationship management are planted.

LEVEL TWO: EXPERTISE AND RELATIONSHIP SKILLS. The actual footwork of relationship management begins at level two. Frequent customer interactions that require the resolution of complex operational or technical issues help build relationship management skills at level two, as illustrated in Figure 12-5. A strong understanding of how to make the firm work for the customer and a commitment to customer success are imperative to progress up the pyramid. Attention to how the firm's products or services can contribute to the wealth-creation processes of the customer will prescribe the speed with which one moves from level two to level three.

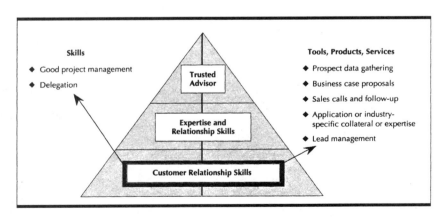

Figure 12-4 *The first level of success in relationship management.*

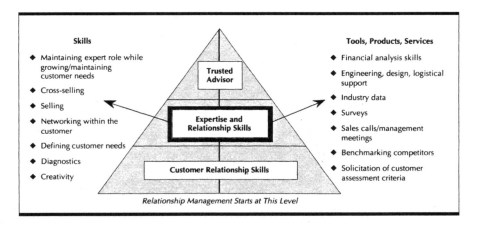

Figure 12-5 *The second level of success in relationship management.*

LEVEL THREE: TRUSTED ADVISOR. The degree of risk and responsibility for the firm's success increases as one moves higher up the pyramid. At level three, trust and leadership dictate the degree of success. Here (see Figure 12-6) one develops a deeper understanding of the firm's expertise, people, product offerings, and processes, and one develops a network within the customer's organization to provide business diagnosis and counsel to top management.

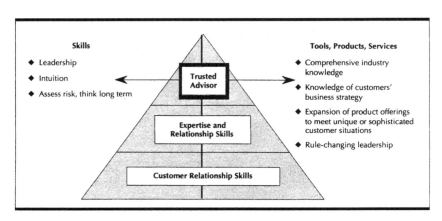

Figure 12-6 *The third level of success in relationship management.*

There are several prerequisites for climbing upward as a relationship manager.

- Individual initiative
- The ability to listen
- Humility—willingness to serve
- Availability to client
- Flexibility—maintaining position of expert while still answering changing client needs
- Sophisticated diagnostic skills
- Investing in the customer's success
  - Professional investment—commitment to finding the best solution and following up on implementation
  - Personal investment—acting on the basis of personal involvement with, and care for, the customer's interests
  - Courage to tackle the tough issues even when the answers may differ with the prevailing opinion in the firm

WHEN IS IT TOO MUCH CHANGE?

A significant part of managing change entails retooling and reeducating the firm's sales and marketing personnel while, at the same time, executives and managers renegotiate performance contracts with all customer-coverage employees. The goal is to have individuals who accept and contribute to the changes required in job configurations, customer mindsets, skills and capabilities, training and development, information flows, and technology needs. Only then can employees be motivated to succeed with new or revised performance measures, recognition programs, incentive plan designs, and performance assessments.

A reengineering effort directed at a group of customer-coverage employees should look at each sales/marketing/service team as if it were a manufacturing plant. How should you reengineer the plant? The human plant?

The impact on compensation—on income dollars—is one way of describing the level of disruption or displacement which might be caused by a reengineering effort. Assume that a 5 percent increase or decrease in income is the point at which an employee's lifestyle or living standard is affected. Introducing a 5 percent change in income across all the personnel who work with customers is sure to impact the customer base. Given that it now takes a much longer time to get to know customers in an in-depth fashion, the possibility of jeopardizing the relationship between the customer base and the customer-coverage personnel of the firm should be carefully considered. Consequently, as the level of impact on employee pay increases, the greater the potential impact on the customer base. A firm should think very carefully about more than a 10 percent change to product quality or production methods.

Whenever an organization ushers in change, it runs the risk of overload, especially if the amount of change being introduced is more than can be managed and processed by the work force. The best way to assess whether the amount of change is manageable is by estimating the impact of the proposed changes on each individual salesperson under various performance scenarios.

THE DISPLACEMENT INDEX

The proprietary statistical model provided in Figure 12-7 generates a set of predictive statistics that gauge the impact that a company's planned change will have on the customer-coverage work force. We have used this displacement model to track the outcomes for over a hundred planned change efforts within sales organizations.

Executives can start by projecting possible outcomes of the planned revisions under historical, year-to-date, or future performance scenarios. To begin, the executive selects a test group of individuals representing various geographic areas, performance levels for sales volume and margin attainment, customer mix, and tenure levels. Next, the executive and the design team calculate the impact of the planned changes at each of the various performance outcomes using a variety of measurement criteria, such as cost of sales, account load per customer team, and pay level attainment per person.

The percent difference between current results and those predicted by the model can be evaluated using the displacement assessment chart shown in Figure 12-7. The model predicts a person's ability to absorb the degree of change and, therefore, whether the planned change is worth the effort. It also forecasts when the degree of change is likely to be perilous for the organization. In such cases, the change should be undertaken only when the business needs are so great that this degree of change is necessary enough to warrant the risk involved.

Several prominent organizations recently have engaged in significant sales-force change efforts that reached the 20 to 25 percent order of magnitude. Certainly, Digital Equipment's

Displacement Index© (Sum of absolute values of old-to-new pay plan changes divided by old pay plan expenditure)	Likely Impact on Sales Force Behavior and Results
Under 10%	Will be regarded as a moderate change. Annual modifications typically fall into this range of displacement, and do not require elaborate implementation planning.
10% to 15%	Behavior will need to change, but not dramatically. Turnover is not a big risk. Some salespeople will be able to take the change in stride. A communication plan becomes important. A transition pay plan may not be necessary (e.g., guarantees to maintain pay at a fixed percentage of prior year earnings, paying the higher of the old and new plans).
15% to 20%	You have the field's careful attention, and they will be concerned. Everyone will have to change somewhat; there is no doubt that things are different. Some people will feel a lot of stress. Some turnover will result unless you have new sales support tools and thorough communications. A transition pay plan is probably required.
20% to 25%	You are pushing the envelope and are in the danger zone. Everyone will experience stress and some turnover is likely, but the program is still feasible. A comprehensive communications effort is essential. Some type of transition pay program will be required.
Over 25%	Don't do it—this amount of change rarely works!

Figure 12-7 *Gauging the impact of change on the sales force.*

introduction of a new sales strategy, a new organization, and a new compensation plan all at once significantly affected sales representatives' behavior, sales results, and potential pay levels. IDS Financial Advisors and Procter & Gamble have also announced major reorganization efforts in an attempt to refocus their go-to-market strategy.

CONCLUSION: MAKING THE RIGHT CHOICES

Throughout this book, we have identified a series of challenges that suppliers face to compete successfully in the global economy of today and tomorrow. Recognizing these challenges and making the hard choices is something that every executive must face.

Some suppliers have already forged the strategic and seamless relationships between buyers and sellers, yet some still rely on the time-worn techniques of coercive selling. Most suppliers are living somewhere between these two extremes, clinging to the edge of their comfort zone and watching trends unfold during this time of rapid change.

For many of these suppliers, inaction will spell disaster. Success will come only to those who make the right choices and step into the spirit of engaging customers. Making the right choices is difficult, given how intractable, demanding, and contradictory many customers can be and considering the variety of evolving procurement capabilities today. It is doubly difficult because each decision must be made relative to the competition and on a customer-by-customer basis, within the specific context of the supplier's resources, its particular customer base, and its unique business objectives.

From our work with clients across North America, we know that the majority of suppliers sense the degree of customer dissatisfaction and feel pressured to make choices and execute decisions. But they are unable to analyze their situation, formulate an explicit strategy, and push forward with an appropriate change process. We wrote this book to guide suppliers through these steps. On the basis of work with clients, we believe that the answers for most suppliers are found by forming customer engagement strategies and using outside-in reengineering efforts to execute those strategies.

THE OPPORTUNITIES FOR CHANGE

Engagement is a complex form of business development. It requires aligning the suppliers' acquisition and distribution processes with a more complete appreciation of customers' procurement processes. Making the alignment and synchronization of activities and outcomes precise enough to successfully differentiate against competition may require formulating engagement strategies on a customer-by-customer basis. The actual nature of the engagement process may vary from customer to customer. It may require dedicated teams equipped to add value during each phase of the engagement process through industry and applications expertise, improved replenishment methods, and broader service solutions.

DOUBLE-CHECKING STRATEGY

The two critical decisions suppliers now face—choosing the right engagement strategy and the best change process to achieve it—involve the whole firm. These decisions are far too large and too important to be left to the sales force alone, or to any other single function.

Choosing the right engagement strategy allows suppliers to align with customers in a way that meets the supplier's profit objectives. As we have detailed in this book, the first step in choosing the right strategy is determining position: understanding the target amount of value that the supplier will add for a customer during the engagement process itself. The second step in perfecting a strategy requires deciding how well the company will execute its position, or how completely it will meet customer expectations, given its position. The third part of the strategy is determining costs: the expense the supplier incurs in executing its position.

All of the value added through the engagement process is added beyond the core product offering; it is value added during the engagement process itself. When the cost and profits from adding this value are calculated and deducted, the remainder represents the contribution that the engagement process makes to the supplier. The supplier can then adjust the inputs, costs, and outcomes of the engagement equation to increase the contribution derived from the engagement process.

As we have detailed throughout the book, making the right choices requires suppliers to:

1. *Understand their customers' procurement capabilities.* Suppliers must listen to their best and most demanding customers with the assumption that all customers will eventually have similar high expectations and reach the same level of purchasing proactivity and sophistication. Understanding today's customers requires recognizing the speed at which and the reasons why customers' procurement capabilities are growing.

2. *Recognize their own strengths and weaknesses in the engagement process.* Every supplier already operates within the framework of engaging customers, by default or by design. Recognizing the de facto strategy and locating its strengths and weaknesses are prerequisites for constructive self-evaluation and change. Suppliers must begin by locating what is broken in their identification, specification, or exchange processes, and then making the decisions necessary to repair them. These decisions may require new organizational struc-

tures, job redesign, customized production lines, delivery terms, installation support, customer training, and/or consultative support services.

3. *Use outside-in, second-generation reengineering tools to design and implement a better engagement strategy.* The tools we provided in Part III will put most suppliers well on their way to organizing the change efforts required to continually improve their customer engagements. These tools describe what it takes to build high-performance teams and contract with employees to complete the organizational change effort. Suppliers can also use the early warning system to monitor trends in their customer bases, operational proficiency, and human capital efficiency.

DOUBLE-CHECKING THE CHANGE PROCESS

With fundamental choices about strategy in place, the supplier can decide which change process is most appropriate. The range of change options—all the way from minor modifications to full-blown reengineering—must be assessed not only in terms of the degree of change needed but the amount of control the supplier wants to maintain, the degree of risk it can tolerate, and the time frames involved.

The powerful but evolutionary approach to reengineering we have introduced in this book can be used to redirect any aspect of the organization that does not contribute to profitable customer relationships. Crucial but often overlooked steps in reengineering include defining the goals and objectives for the change process and exploring all of the possible means to those ends. The second-generation form of reengineering described here builds those crucial steps into the reengineering process, and includes steps for designing the process, setting an appropriate time frame, and establishing measures for ongoing monitoring and improvement.

The comprehensive organizational realignment often dictated by a new engagement strategy and the reengineering required to achieve it may generate companywide change that affects virtually every function and every employee. Managing that change and staying on top of the human element is one of the greatest challenges executives will face in the coming years. They must be able to fill the gap between long-term planning exercises and the rudimentary day-to-day realities of meeting monthly business plans.

The needs and trends discussed in this book will not disappear within the next few years; they will continue to grow well into the next century. The increasingly sophisticated demands of buyers will continue to shake out the number of suppliers that are able and willing to meet buyers' needs. When customers find suppliers that meet their criteria, they will form the long-term relationships that eliminate competing suppliers.

From the supplier's perspective, the stakes associated with these trends could not be higher. Those who survive into the next century will be the ever-smaller number of firms that make the right choices about strategy and change in response to ever-better procurement capability and global competition.

INDEX

Note: The *n*. after a page number refers to a note.

Cross-functional disconnect, 116–117
Cross-functional organization, 109
Cross-functional teams (*see* Teams, cross-
  functional customer-coverage)
Customer relationship management, 106,
  126–127
  importance of, 2–4
  skills for, 235–238
Customer satisfaction:
  in exchange processes, 134–138
  marketing and, 18
  measurements of, 138, 170–172
Customers:
  buying trends of, 178–179
  communications technology and,
    21–22
  as inherently messy, 5, 116
  long-term value demanded by, 30–32
  procurement capabilities of, 1–2,
    177–178
  retention of, 176–177
  targeting profiles of, 122–123
  team approach demanded by, 75–76
  training and education for, 137–138
  value added expected by, 29
  (*See also* Procurement)
Customization:
  mass marketing vs., 18, 114, 116
  product design and, 137

Dartnel surveys, 73
Delivery methods, 137
  dock-to-stock, 30, 39
Dell Computer, 107, 154, 156
Design teams (*see* Teams, design)
Digital Equipment Corp. (DEC), 95–96,
  100–101, 240–241
Direct mail, 107–108, 121
Disconnects, 111–140
  cross-functional, 116–117
  defined, 112
  functional excellence as, 112–113
  mass markets orientation as, 113–116
Displacement index, 239–241
Distribution channels, 76, 107–108,
  121–122
Dock-to-stock delivery, 30, 39
Downsizing, 199

Drucker, Peter F., 80, 95, 112

Early warning systems, 175–185
  for buying trends, 178–179
  capabilities indicators in, 177–178
  for competitive strength, 179
  customer stability indicators in,
    176–179
  development of, 182–185
  for financial stability, 180
  for human capital efficiency, 181
  for operational proficiency, 179–181
  purpose of, 175
Eastman Kodak, 33
EDI, 22, 23, 25, 30, 31, 139–140
Education, 137–138
E. F. Hutton, 72, 100
Efficiency buy, 52
80/20 rule, 27
Electronics technology, 21–22
Enduring return, 162–164
  external indicators for, 166–167
  internal indicators for, 165–166
  personal contributions to, 167–172
Engagement, theory of the, 95
Engagement equation, 94–95, 146–148
Engagement era, 91–110
  defined, 91–92
  evolution of, 91–92
  tailored product offerings in, 104–106
Engagement managers, 126–127, 133
Engagement potential, 117–134
  in exchange processes, 134–140
  in identification processes, 117–125
  in specification processes, 126–134
Engagement process:
  contribution in, 101–102
  cost in, 99–101
  defined, 91–92
  effectiveness of, 164–167
  execution in, 96–98
  measurements for, 164–167
  position in, 95–96
  value in, 98–99
Engagement strategy, 102–104, 141–157
  base case for, 148–149
  choice of, 244–246
  for competitiveness, 150–151